The Corporal and the Celestials

The Corporal and the Celestials

*In north China with the 1st Battalion,
Royal Inniskilling Fusiliers, 1909–1912*

Text and photographs by **James Hutchinson**

Edited by **Bill Jackson**

Foreword by **Keith Jeffery**

Historical introduction by **Michael Bosworth**

ULSTER HISTORICAL FOUNDATION

FOR MATTHEW

In affectionate remembrance of his great-grandfather

Ulster Historical Foundation would like
to thank the Taoiseach's Office, Dublin,
the Trustees of the Regimental Museum
of the Royal Inniskilling Fusiliers, the
Belfast Natural History and Philosophical
Society, Gladys McFerran née Hutchinson
and family and Mrs. Muriel Bell for
financial assistance

Published by Ulster Historical Foundation

First published 2008

© Ulster Historical Foundation, Unit 7, Cotton Court, Waring Street,
Belfast BT1 2ED, Northern Ireland, and Bill Jackson

ISBN 978-1-903688-63-2

Designed by Bob Elliott

Typeset in Miller by Hope Services (Abingdon) Ltd

Printed in England by Cromwell Press, Trowbridge, Wiltshire

Contents

Foreword BY KEITH JEFFERY   vii

Preface BY BILL JACKSON   ix

Historical introduction BY MICHAEL BOSWORTH   xiii

   Prelude   1
   Crete   2
   Malta   4

1 *Voyage*
   From Malta to China, September to November 1909   9
   Suez Canal   10
   The Red Sea   12
   Indian Ocean   15
   Ceylon   15
   The Straits of Malacca   17
   Singapore   18
   The China Seas   18
   Hong Kong   20
   The China Coast   23

2 *The Battalion in north China*   27
   Sports   32
   An unusual route march   35

3 *Tientsin*   37
   The Concessions   37
   The Native City   42

4 *Peking*   50
   The City Walls   52
   The Foreign Legations   55
   The Tartar City   63
   The Imperial City   69
   The Forbidden City   70
   The Temple of Heaven   74
   Ascending the throne   79
   Other temples and sights of Peking   81

5   *Manners and customs of the Chinese*   92
      Government   97
      Education   100
      Pidgin English   105

6   *The great sights of China*   109
      The Imperial Summer Palace   109
      The Peking to Kalgan Railway and the Great Wall of China   113
      The Ming Tombs   118

7   *Eventful times*   121
      Summer Camp   121
      Revolution   123
      On detachment in Wei-Hai-Wei   130
      Departure   138

Postscript   139

General index of English terms   142

Index of Chinese proper names   144

Foreword

'JOIN the army and see the world' used to be one of the advertising slogans for recruitment into the British armed forces, and in the days when Britain's imperial and international interests meant that peace-time garrisons were maintained across the globe, hundreds of thousands of young men from Ireland and Britain travelled from the familiar shores of home to exotic spots across the earth. Few of those soldiers can so vividly and excitingly have preserved that experience for us as did the Inniskilling Fusilier James Hutchinson whose sharply-observed narrative and marvellous photographs have valuably been assembled by Bill Jackson in this wonderful book.

There is fascination in every page of the volume. At Singapore on the journey out east, Hutchinson noted that one could acquire a walking stick 'according to taste from the reed-like cane of the sentimental swell to the strong shillelagh-like bludgeon, which would be useful for an Irish fair, or a garrotting attack', an observation which perhaps reveals as much about Hutchinson himself as it does about retail opportunities in Singapore. His curiosity is unbounded and encompasses Confucian temples, Chinese education, shop signs, 'Pidgin English' and 'many queer kinds of food', adding that, among the smaller mammals eaten, 'black cats and dogs are considered the best'.

While the tone of Hutchinson's text is predominantly one of an interested spectator, fascinated by the Orient and the strangeness of his situation, there are hints, too, of the imperial relationship and the subservient position of the local inhabitants. Noting that pilfering was rife among the Chinese, and punishment by flogging frequent, he recorded that Sergeant Gallagher 'invariably carried out such punishment', but 'for fear of retaliation from the Chinese outside, he seldom left the barracks'. During the 'eventful times' of the 1911 revolution, too, there were fears that the Inniskillings might have to be deployed to protect the foreign concessions in north China.

Bill Jackson and the Ulster Historical Foundation are to be congratulated for bringing James Hutchinson's evocative words and pictures to the wider public which they so clearly deserve. The photographs are but a sample of the collection held at the regimental museum and it is to be hoped that increasing numbers of people will exploit this precious resource which itself abundantly complements the (perhaps unexpectedly) rich archives of Chinese material held by other local institutions such as Queen's University Belfast and the Ulster Museum. Scholars already come to Belfast to study late nineteenth and early twentieth-century China. Now they will have to add Enniskillen to their itineraries.

KEITH JEFFERY

Queen's University Belfast
2007

Preface

OVER fifty years ago, as he was nearing his seventies, James Hutchinson gave me some 250 lantern slides, 150 postcard-size photographic negatives, notebooks containing manuscripts, three maps and some coins on a string. Virtually all related to his time in China as a soldier in the Inniskillings. He was the much-esteemed Honorary Treasurer of my father's Ballywalter, Co. Down parish. I was seventeen and Hutchinson had recognised that I was intrigued by anything to do with other countries and their peoples.

The three heavy boxes of three-and-a-quarter by three-and-a-quarter-inch glass slides accompanied me through much of my own widely-travelled career – much to my wife's chagrin, since I never did anything with them. I had, however, promised myself that doing 'something' with them and with the manuscripts, to repay what I had regarded as a debt of honour, would be a first call as soon as I had time. That promise I have now finally been able to keep, in my own retirement.

Sadly, James Hutchinson died in 1963, so that I could not consult him further: but working on the project has brought me into touch again with his daughter and her family. It is primarily for them and for the fine Regimental Museum of the Royal Inniskilling Fusiliers in Enniskillen that I have undertaken the task. The family have known that he was an exceptional human being, and already a great-grandson has taken a keen interest in him. For its part, the Museum exists to perpetuate the memory of one of the great regiments. These are surely the two key requirements if heritage is not to be lost to sight: that individuals and institutions alike determine to conserve what has survived from the past, and from time to time revive and re-live it.

James Hutchinson was born in 1886. He came from Coolbanagher near Portarlington in County Laois, Queen's County as it was then. His formal education stopped on leaving school at fourteen. Career prospects being slight in the Ireland of those days, many young men understandably looked to the British army for the chance of travel, adventure and fulfilment. He enlisted a little over 100 years ago. The barstool and the billiard cue were not for him in leisure time: indeed, he worked in the temperance cause. Rather, Hutchinson was avid to learn about the people of China, 'the Celestials' as they styled themselves, and later, to communicate what he had seen and learnt to all whom he subsequently met. In fact, there proved to be no less than six neat longhand manuscripts, although none written with publication in mind. They overlap significantly and I have edited them into one narrative. Readers will readily detect that they were essentially commentaries to his lecture presentations based on the lantern slides.

An unquenchable curiosity characterises Hutchinson's writings and his photographs, a curiosity which resembles nothing so much as that of the great traveller and father of history, Herodotus. Both actively wanted to see and experience the unfamiliar: Hutchinson is disappointed that the forecast typhoon fails to hit the troopship. Both were also circumspect – they knew when they didn't *know*, and didn't hide the fact. He states, for example 'Here I see many who are pure Chinese in features and costume, but their caste or rank I have no power of estimating'.

Hutchinson was a non-commissioned officer. So one should not expect a major-general's analysis of military strategies. Nor a retired ambassador's thesis on the rights or wrongs of Great Power policies towards a China emerging into the 20th century. Nonetheless, he could recognise what he saw for what it was, and even Mao-Tse-Tung probably never put it more bluntly: 'The roads, bridges and great walls of these towns all tell of a time when there was a government in the country which did something; their present condition tells of a government which is defunct, and only waits its time to be removed'.

What we *do* have is China quite simply as Hutchinson saw it: its landscapes and peoples, and in particular the great cultural land-marks of Peking and Tientsin. And a glimpse – if not of an United Nations in embryo – at least of a significant number of the Great Powers acting in tandem to protect their interests.

Not many soldiers of the modest rank of Corporal (later to become Acting Company Quarter-Master Sergeant) can have left a record such as this. Fewer still with the grasp and unexpected erudition which Hutchinson brought to bear. And of those few, surely none who simultaneously captured all he saw with the camera, in the still relatively early days of photography.

He put together an album of 202 photographs for the Regiment, presented to the Museum by his widow. He speaks of 600 slides in all, of which only some 250 survive, and he noted that 152 negatives were missing – they 'had to be dumped periodically owing to weight and space'. That is a pity, but we can be thankful that the great majority of slides, negatives and prints which have survived are not only technically competent but wonderfully illustrative. This from a man who had only taken up the hobby in Crete two years earlier, when he got hold of a box camera.

In China, he says, he became more proficient, on 'securing a film Kodak from a Chinaman who apparently did not understand it'. He describes only briefly the immense difficulties under which he had to labour. No films at first, only glass plates; no darkroom, only camp washrooms; no colour photography of course – so he hand-tinted dozens of the slides, some of which appear in a centre-spread. The odd blemish of focus or exposure is well outweighed by the overall impact. The envelopes remain in which he purchased his photographic papers: Ilford P.O.P. (Printing Out Paper), 'glossy mauve'; Ilford's Hyptona Self-Toning Paper (Collodion) in Tropical Packing; Kodak Limited of London's Velox ('Open in yellow or very subdued daylight – Directions enclosed' at one shilling for eleven sheets; and Illingworth's Slogas Gaslight Paper – 'vigorous glossy' and 'with exceptional latitude'.

The context of his time in China is the Great Power Concessions in Tientsin and the foreign Legations in Peking, which were to be protected following the murderous Boxer Rebellion of 1900. Michael Bosworth, a student of that period who resided in Peking in the 1980s and 1990s, has encouraged me throughout and has very helpfully written a short historical introduction to put the Inniskillings' mission in perspective. Professor Keith Jeffery, who kindly recommended to the Ulster Historical Foundation that the work was worthy of publication, has contributed a Foreword.

James Hutchinson's writing must of course be seen in the setting of his time. His style can be laborious by comparison with today's. There are passages when he is far from 'politically correct'. He refers to 'the pigtail race', criticises – but makes use of – the venality of temple guards, berates the corruption of the Manchu Empire, and with jingoist emotion writes of 'the dear old Union Jack'. But he equally sincerely highlights the virtues of his hosts and their ancient civilisation – the astonishing monuments, the incredible feats of engineering, the high culture – and makes some comparisons to the disadvantage of us supposedly civilised Europeans. It goes without saying that the China of 1909–12 is far from the China of 2007, four generations on.

At times his insights will resonate more with a British readership, at others with an Irish. The Emperor's court procedures would not go down well with George V in Windsor Castle, he feels. But the T'angshan railway yards remind him of Dublin's Inchicore and he describes a weapon as a 'strong shillelagh-like bludgeon'. Quite apart from the man's achievement, I found in that British/Irish duality a further dimension to his story, which added to my enthusiasm to place his work on public record. It had occurred to me only in recent years to wonder why a man with such a pronounced Leinster brogue should have spent the greater part of his life in *Northern* Ireland. His wife Emily's accent was virtually impenetrable in our Ards Peninsula! My abiding memory is of them in their bungalow, Emily forever laughing, Jim chuckling rheumily and tamping the tobacco in his pipe, held deftly in the crook of the thumb which the Germans and Turks at Gallipoli had left turned permanently inward.

It turned out as I had suspected: the family had moved in 1924, some time after rebels in the civil war which followed Ireland's Independence had come to their farm at dead of night and demanded transport to make a quick getaway. Luckily Hutchinson had stripped the car down and it was in bits on the garage floor. However, those were times in which it was ill seen by some that an Irishman should have taken His Britannic Majesty's shilling. The Hutchinsons headed north. The better part of a century on, it may or may not be accurate to see them as having been refugees: at the time it may largely have been a decision in favour of better prospects of employment.

In China, as in Ireland and so many other countries, foreign domination over decades or centuries served only to widen and deepen fissures that already existed among the population. Today, thankfully, there are wider horizons: a Chinese Embassy in Dublin and an Irish one in Beijing; both countries in membership of the United Nations; a fresh impulse towards reconciliation in Ireland, towards cross-Border and all-Ireland activities; and new freedom for tourists from China to visit the West. Nothing would please me more than to see this memoir attract as much attention in Hutchinson's native Laois as in Fermanagh or Down, to see his photographs displayed not just alongside the records of comrades-in-arms in Enniskillen, but also more widely in Ireland north and south. And perhaps even in China, where, understandably, the period of foreign occupations and concessions is hardly the one on which they look back with most pleasure or pride.

Finally, I personally am anything but an expert on either China or its last days an as empire. So, I have taken Hutchinson's texts as I found them and very largely retained the sequence and spelling which he used, tidying up only a handful of minor inconsistencies and factual errors.

In completing this labour of love, I warmly acknowledge the encouragement and support given me by James Hutchinson's daughter, Mrs Gladys McFerran, and her family; Michael Bosworth's invaluable help on orthography and on the history of the period; the help and partial sponsorship of the Trustees of the Regimental Museum and Major Jack Dunlop and Major George Stephens MBE DL, respectively the present and former Curator; the enthusiasm of the Executive Director of the Ulster Historical Foundation, Fintan Mullan, on seeing the photographs; my wife Maggie's forbearance down the years, the contributions of my aunt Muriel Bell and of the Belfast Natural History and Philosophical Society to the project and our son Dr. Nick Jackson's skilled and patient work in scanning the negatives, prints and lantern slides.

BILL JACKSON

Wheatley, Oxfordshire
September 2007

Historical introduction

As a student since my college and university days of China's history and international relations since 1840, I was both intrigued and excited when Bill Jackson first introduced me to the slides, negatives, and texts he had received from James Hutchinson. Having visited Tientsin (Tianjin) and Peking (Beijing) many times in the 1980s and having resided in Peking from 1990–1994, I had made a point of taking long walks through some of the former concession areas in Tientsin and the old Legation Quarter in Peking. At times I even snapped a few photos just like Mr. Hutchinson did.

I thoroughly enjoyed viewing the photographic treasure that Bill had faithfully and carefully preserved and was immediately of the opinion that the work required to get both text and images into the public domain would be well worth the effort. I was also honored with Bill's invitation to prepare this brief preface as a way of providing some historical context to the Hutchinson legacy.

When James Hutchinson arrived in North China in late 1909, the Manchu Ch'ing (Qing) Dynasty and the ancient imperial system of government in China were on the verge of total collapse. The revolution of October 10, 1911, which led to the abdication of the last emperor, P'u-Yi, and the establishment of a Republic, was less than two years away. The Chinese Empire lay prostrate before the military might and economic ambitions of the Western Powers and Japan. These countries were still in the midst of imperialistic competition for territory, markets, new sources of raw materials, etc.

The danger of the implosion of Chinese self-government and the wholesale carving-up of the Empire had grown rapidly from 1895 on. Japan defeated China on the battlefield and obtained control over Taiwan in 1895. Germany's seizure of Kiaochow Bay (Jiaozhouwan) and the surrounding area in 1897 set off a scramble for similar coastal leaseholds among other powers. In 1898, Russia gained control of Port Arthur (today Lüshun), France acquired Kuangchouwan in the far south, and Britain acquired both Weihaiwei in Shandong Province and the New Territories neighboring their colony of Hong Kong. In addition, Chinese influence in Korea was officially ended as a result of the 1904–5 Russo-Japanese war (which saw Japan seize Port Arthur from the Russians).

These new areas of foreign control in China were in addition to the various foreign settlements and 'concessions' already existing in cities such as Shanghai, Tientsin, and Canton (Guangzhou). In most of these areas foreigners were not subject to Chinese law, while Christian missionaries took advantage of the foreign ascendancy to target the interior of the country. In the process they confronted age-old Chinese beliefs and customs with a strange new religion.

Needless to say, numerous Chinese citizens felt a deep humiliation at the impotence of their government in the face of this loss of land and sovereignty. Many felt ill-treated or exploited by the 'foreign devils'. Trouble began to brew in 1898–1899 as various secret societies and other patriotic groups began to engage in acts of violence against foreigners and their interests, beginning in the vicinity of the German concession in Shandong. Many, especially missionaries, their families and Chinese converts, were murdered. To add to the tension, the reform-minded emperor Kuang Hsü had been imprisoned in 1898 by his aunt, the reactionary and anti-foreign Empress Dowager.

By June 1900, one of these groups, known in the West as 'Boxers', had begun to infiltrate Peking. These practitioners of martial arts believed that they could obtain magical powers making them impervious to Western bullets. Following the murder of a Japanese diplomat and the German ambassador, the diplomatic and missionary population of the capital (supported by small contingents of marines from several countries) found themselves under siege in the Legation Quarter. The Empress Dowager, fearing the threat of this radical movement to her own legitimacy and power, threw her weight behind the Boxers and supported a declaration of war against the Western nations and Japan. Fortunately for those besieged behind the walls of the Legation Quarter, most of the Imperial Chinese troops did not support the fanatical Boxers in a full-scale assault. It appears many of the Chinese civilian and military authorities, doubtful of the wisdom of the 'declaration of war', dragged their feet or ignored orders from the Empress Dowager's court. Finally, an allied force consisting mainly of Japanese, British, Russian, American, and French troops entered Peking on August 14, 1900, liberating the surviving foreign population and Chinese Christian converts.

The Empress Dowager and her court fled the capital, while the foreign troops went on a looting spree, helping themselves to art works and other booty. Some allied troops, especially the Russians in Manchuria and the late arriving Germans in and around Peking, carried-out punitive 'mopping up' campaigns. Ostensibly aimed at rooting out remaining Boxers, these turned into violent and bloody assaults on whole towns and villages. Many innocent people were killed. To add to the Chinese humiliation, an allied victory parade was held in the Imperial City itself.

One year later, on September 7, 1901, a peace treaty between China and the foreign powers was finally signed. The terms of importance to us as we consider the Hutchinson text and photographs are as follows:

- The Legation Quarter in Peking was to be placed under foreign control. This included the right to fortify the area and post troops for the protection of the embassies.

- Twelve spots between Peking and the coast were to be garrisoned by the Powers. This was to ensure secure communications between the Legations and naval vessels visiting coastal waters. This implied effective foreign control over the train line running from Peking southwest to Tientsin, and then again northwards to Shanhaikwan (Shanhaiguan) via the port of Ch'inhuangtao (Qinhuangdao).

As a direct consequence of these terms, James Hutchinson and his First Battalion, Royal Inniskilling Fusiliers were posted to North China from 1909–1912. Looking at the historical timeframe, he arrived only eight years after the Boxer peace treaty had been signed. The Ch'ing Dynasty would see its final collapse during this time, with the Wu-Ch'ang (Wuchang) uprising of October 10, 1911, leading to the abdication of the last emperor, P'u-Yi, on February 12, 1912. When Hutchinson departed China that November, the new, but shaky, Republic of China was governing the country.

Hutchinson's observations and photographs cover primarily the Concession areas and native city of Tientsin, the Legation Quarter and the city of Peking, some spots in the environs of Peking, Shanhaikwan, and the British Territory of Weihaiwei in Shandong Province. At this time the Boxer 'troubles' were surely still fresh in the memories of foreigners and Chinese alike. The Legation Quarter in Peking had been restructured and fortified, and foreign garrisons patrolled the various areas as allowed under the treaty.

During the three years he served in north China, Hutchinson did not see any military action. Thus he had spare time on his hands, and fortunately for us he made the best of it. Not only did he take the initiative and leave the barracks to see the country around him, he also brought his powers of observation and his camera. His photographs, especially those of everyday Chinese and their lives, are of historical value as they show the country in the extreme twilight of imperial rule. Although an unknown on the China scene compared to such western photographers as John Thomson before him and Sidney Gamble after him, we are indeed privileged to have these valuable records of a time (and in some cases places) gone by.

Hutchinson, in his writing, proves to be very observant (and at times to show very strong opinions). For a soldier of occupation, he proves to be open-minded and eager to learn about the ancient culture all around him. At some points it is clear that he has taken pains to go into some detail on a particular subject. Although there are some errors when it comes to historical facts, he seems to have kept fairly well informed about the momentous events occurring around him.

Our thanks should go to James Hutchinson for providing us with these fascinating images of the China of a century ago. Due to the efforts of Bill Jackson, and with the support of the Regimental Museum in Ireland, the public and scholars of the period will have these previously unpublished photographs for their research and enjoyment.

I should add a brief note about the romanization of Chinese names and places. It was agreed that the Wade-Giles romanization system, prevalent at the time, be selected for use in this book. Although some scholars might disapprove of this and prefer the use of Pinyin, we wished the text to remain as faithful as possible to the original. Hutchinson wrote using Wade-Giles with varying degrees of accuracy. His practice of placing hyphens between each Chinese sound has also been retained, although this does not conform exactly to the rules of Wade-Giles.

Regarding my assistance with issues concerning historical accuracy, I have attempted to point out any errors or areas where clarification might be required. In some cases this supplemental information will appear in the form of some of the footnotes to the text. Of course, any errors in this regard are solely my responsibility.

MICHAEL BOSWORTH

Vientiane, Laos
2006

Prelude

THE battalion was stationed at Ebrington Barracks, Londonderry, when I enlisted in the Royal Inniskilling Fusiliers on 2nd September 1905. After the usual course of recruit training at the Depot, Omagh, my squad joined the battalion which had then moved to Victoria Barracks, Belfast. When I joined, little did I think that in the near future I should be privileged with a tour to the far East and various countries between. As a soldier I did not expect to do all my service at home, and as I had always an ambition to travel, the fact that we were now under orders for Crete was to my satisfaction.

It was on the 12th February 1907 that the battalion under the command of Lt. Col. C. J. L. Davidson D.S.O. (who had just assumed command) with Capt R. C. Smythe, Adjutant, and Regimental Sergeant Major Guy Bleakley left Belfast en route for Crete – an island in the Mediterranean Sea. Belfast on this occasion presented an animated scene. The streets were lined with people as the battalion marched through en route to the quay, all taking a last glimpse of the favourite regiment of the North and many bidding farewell to sons, brothers and friends who were now to leave them – perhaps never to return. As the *S.S. Antrim* sailed from the quay with the battalion on

Quite probably with Hutchinson among them, the Inniskillings parade at Victoria Barracks on 18 June 1906
From the album of Col. W. H. Crawford, Regimental Museum of the Royal Inniskilling Fusiliers, Enniskillen

board, crowds of people who had lined the quay on all sides showed their appreciation and love for the regiment by cheering and waving handkerchiefs, which was duly responded to by our band playing the popular air of 'Auld Lang Syne'.

After a very rough passage across the channel, Heysham was reached about 1 a.m. the following morning, from where we entrained to Southampton and embarked on the *Hired Transport Sicilia* and were sailing about 5 p.m. After about two hours' sail from Southampton the steamer dropped anchor and remained for the night in order to have daylight to ensure a safe passage though the 'Needles'. At daybreak she sailed slowly through the dangerous zone, after which she regained full speed and ploughed the 'deep' in excellent manner until the Bay of Biscay was reached.

We arrived in Gibraltar on 17th, where a small detachment of the Royal Garrison Artillery disembarked. We had just time to view the high rocks surrounding the harbour, when the ship sailed again into the straits and entered the Mediterranean Sea next day. The voyage through the Mediterranean we rather enjoyed, it being very calm. Various sports were introduced on board, which helped to pass away the time until our arrival at Malta on 21st, where we anchored in the Grand Harbour for some hours to take on stores etc. Leaving Malta and after a pleasant voyage, we arrived at Candia, Crete, on the 24th February and disembarked the following day, thus completing the voyage from Southampton in 11 days.

Crete

It may be of interest to mention why British troops at that time were stationed in Crete. The island of Crete belongs to Greece. Its inhabitants are mostly Turks and it is owing to this that so much trouble prevails. The Turks being Mahomedans and the Greeks Christians, they cannot agree and bloodshed often ensued. Again, the Mahomedans do not like the idea of being ruled by the Greek nation. Turkey threatened to take the island off Greece altogether. Greece being only a small nation and not able to cope with the conquering Turk, applied to the foreign powers to police the island on her behalf. England, France, Italy and Russia answered her call and placed troops on the island, the British making their headquarters at Candia, while Russia, Italy and France protected Canea, the capital.[1]

---

[1] Nuttall's 1907 Encyclopaedia of General Knowledge described the situation in the following terms: 'in nominal subjection to Turkey after 1669', Crete had been 'in perpetual revolt. The rising of 1895 led to the intervention of the great powers of Europe, and the Turkish troops having been withdrawn in 1898 under pressure from Great Britain, Russia, France, and Italy, Prince George of Greece was appointed High Commissioner, ruling on behalf of these powers.'

The arrival of the Inniskillings in Crete

Candia was the commercial town, whilst Canea was the capital. F Company went on detachment to Canea where French troops were also stationed. Our quarters here were composed of wooden huts placed at intervals along the top of the old ramparts on the north and west side of the town.

There were practically no serious incidents during our stay on the island. Duty was light, apart from the usual guards, town picquets, drill parades, route marches and general training. As our role here consisted of policing the town, picquets, accompanied occasionally by a Gendarme, were always on duty.

The climate was very hot in summer and mild in winter. Fruit was in abundance, especially the grape. 'Veno', the fermented juice of the grape, was the native beverage. Stored in skins, this sweet wine was not only to be had in towns and villages but appeared to be peddled around the country. Very cheap it was too. So cheap that one could get intoxicated for less than a shilling. In spite of this, it was surprising that drunkenness among the troops was comparatively light. Perhaps the vigil of our Provost Sergeant, Sgt. now Major Maguire, was the deterrent.

Sport consisted mainly of Inter Company football and cross country running. Swimming also was popular and many learned to swim in Crete.

Regimental Sergeant Major Bleakley retired when we left Crete. C/Sgt. Framingham was appointed in his stead and promoted later in Malta to R.S.M.

A nuisance in camp was the wild or stray dogs which roved around at night after swill. The Provost Sergeant soon put paid to most of them. He secured a sporting shot gun and practically every night, especially moonlit nights, the camp would be awakened by a bang followed by the pitiful yelping of a victim.

In a sense Crete was a lonely station after the excitement of Belfast. It was certainly lonely for the married personnel who had left their families behind. There were many interesting places to visit, especially the old buried city of Knossos. To get around it was advisable to hire a donkey. Many men took up hobbies to while away their spare time.

It was here that I thought of photography. I got hold of a box camera for a few shillings to start with. Later I picked up an old German-made camera and tripod. Plates and material in general were difficult to obtain. However I fished out sufficient to give me a start. I picked up the art after some time, but there were many snags. Photography then was different from now. Glass plates were the only medium (no films). One had to do his developing under a barrack room table covered over with blankets. All negatives, being on glass, had to be dumped on moving owing to weight and bulk.

Malta

After one year's service in Candia, Crete, we sailed for Malta on 25th February 1908 in the *Troopship Soudan*, arriving in the Grand Harbour on 28th. This was only a short voyage but very rough, and our steamer took great delight in riding the waves, which caused her to dip occasionally and made many passengers sea-sick. After three days' sail Malta was reached and the anchor was dropped in the Grand Harbour. We disembarked and marched to Verdella Barracks where we were stationed until early the following year, when we moved to St Andrews Barracks, Pembroke.

A reader who may have visited Malta will have some idea of the island's layout. There are two splendid harbours with Valletta perched high up in the middle. The island is in reality one huge rock, the soil thereon being largely imported. Were it not for the forces, both Naval and Military, the Maltese would find their means of livelihood meagre indeed, for there are few industries on the island.

The three principal Infantry Barracks are St Andrews, Imtarfa and Verdella. We took over Verdella Barracks on arrival. This barracks being situated on the side of the Grand Harbour, it was necessary to cross the Grand Harbour by ferry steamer to get to Valletta. As these ceased running at 10.30 p.m., should one be in Valletta after that hour, he would either have to cross over by rowing boat or hire a 'Carrozza' cab and travel overland behind the harbour to reach Verdella, the journey being about three miles.

Malta proved a vast change from our lonely station in Crete. Plenty of duties but also abundance of sport and competitions for here was a strongly garrisoned island and the headquarters of our Mediterranean fleet. H.R.H. the Duke of Connaught was Governor[2] at the time, and very active he was, keeping everyone on their toes. Shortly after our arrival we took part with other units in a General Officer Commanding's Inspection and March Past. In brigade orders the following day the G.O.C. in commenting on the turnout etc unfavourably, criticised the Inniskillings. He stated that in marching past they appeared to be 'sorefooted and weary'. Such criticism came as a 'bombshell' to all ranks. All Officers, N.C.Os and men felt the criticism terribly, especially our Commanding Officer, Adjutant & R.S.M. The C.O. literally 'flared'. However as it turned out later, it was a blessing in disguise, for it gave such a fillip to all ranks that before we finally left Malta the G.O.C. not only apologised but admitted that the Inniskillings were one of the 'finest' that ever came under his command.

And no wonder. Both in training, manoeuvres and especially in the field of sport, the Battalion just won all in front of them. We won practically every trophy in Malta, taking most with us to China. Whether it was for shooting, football, rowing, running or swimming, we always came out on top. The men used to boast about the extra guards they had to find, to guard all these cups etc in the Library.

We were only a few months at Verdella when we transferred to St Andrews. This was a more modern barracks, more central, and being just beside the rifle range at Pembroke gave us an opportunity for convenient rifle practice. Our final victory in Malta was the winning of the Royal Army Temperance Association 'All Army' Shooting Shield in 1909. Although we had not the result of this competition before we left Malta, all ranks, especially our C.O. were elated when news finally reached us in Tientsin that we had bagged this shield also. I was proud to have been a member of that team.

We had our Annual Sports at St Andrews. As the families were now with us, provision for their entertainment was not overlooked. Sergeant Leo Burnett, Corporal C. Irwin and Private Stevenson, as comedians gave them ample fun as Suffragettes etc.

When we came to Verdella, our first task was to convert the splendid gymnasium there into a theatre. We erected a stage and provided the

---

[2] H.R.H. Prince Arthur, Duke of Connaught and Strathearn, 1850–1942, was High Commissioner and Commander-in-Chief, Mediterranean from 1907 till 1911.

canvas which Lance Corporal Lunn and some helpers painted. This L/Cpl was no mean artist and the scenery he painted did him credit. I shall always remember his front drop screen depicting the Battle of 'Peter's Hill'[3]. Talent there was in plenty: it only needed fishing out.

We found many splendid comedians in the ranks. Corporal Irwin, as an impersonator of Harry Lauder, was magnificent. (He purchased his discharge in 1910 to take up the stage as a career). We ran many good plays, usually of the humorous type. I actually saw our C.O. literally fall off his seat one night, so heartily did he laugh. Benefit concerts were a speciality and we raised many hundreds of pounds whether for a widow and children whose husband had died, or other deserving causes. We were not long at Verdella when a terrible disaster to the *S.S. Sardinia* occurred. She went on fire in the harbour and was sailed out immediately in case of danger to other shipping and ran aground quite near Verdella. Her crew, mostly Arabs it appears, were in the habit of cooking on deck. Some of their burning fuel fell into the hold and set the ship alight. It was pitiful to watch these poor wretches clinging to the side of that red hot and flaming ship[4].

The Emperor of Germany paid an official visit in May 1909. His Royal Yacht the *Hohenzollern* sailed into the Grand Harbour early in the forenoon. Strada Reale and Floriana were lined by troops, with a Guard of Honour at the Governor's palace. Although all warships were decorated in his honour, all forts and guns guarding the Harbour were camouflaged just in case His Imperial Majesty and suite might do a little spying. We had also in the same year an unofficial visit from H.M. King Edward VII, a brother to H.R.H. Duke of Connaught, the Governor.

I did not go in for making lantern slides until I went to China, apart from a few amateurish ones in Malta. Photography was difficult in the Army: amenities were the trouble and the nearest suitable place was an ablution room – even there water was scarce. There were also difficulties in the way of a dark room for developing etc. In China I became more proficient after securing a film Kodak (postcard size) from a Chinaman who apparently did not understand it. My hobby had at last become more successful and I enjoyed it. In China too I became acquainted with a Chinese photographer who contracted to do all my developing and printing at a very cheap rate.

I regret now that I did not at the time make more slides and pictures of incidents connected with the Battalion, especially in Malta and China. When I went to China I concentrated more on the country and its customs, with the result that I have a large collection of slides on China.

---

[3] Fought in 1900 in the Second Anglo-Boer War.

[4] The *S.S. Sardinia* caught fire just outside Grand Harbour and was run ashore on rocks off Fort Ricasoli. Of twelve saloon passengers two died, together with sixteen crew. There were also 142 Arabs on deck, of whom many lost their lives.

Shortly after arrival in Crete we instituted a Regimental Lodge of the International Order of Good Templars. Through this medium and the Royal Army Temperance Association I became an enthusiastic worker in the temperance cause. Our Lodge was a very 'happy' family indeed and nothing during my service did I enjoy more than the comradeship of this Lodge and its happy band of members. In Malta, where many similar naval and military lodges existed, we enjoyed visiting them on most nights of the week. This comradeship and brotherhood, if you like, existed and continued right on to the battlefield of Gallipoli[5], where we continued to hold lodge meetings even under fire. Alas, however, many of my most intimate comrades were killed in that first world war.

[5] See Postscript.

1 Voyage
From Malta to China, September to November 1909

On the 24th September 1909 we embarked on the *Hired Transport Soudan* (which belongs to the P. & O. Steamship company) at Malta for a voyage to the Far East. We had been stationed in Malta for one year and seven months and were now on our way to do a short term of service in North China, our next station being Tientsin.

It was not long before Malta was out of sight and looking over the rails we found ourselves in the centre of an enormous circle of water. Not even a small sailing vessel bespeckled that blue circle and very few vessels came in sight. Land was not again seen until we came near the coast of Egypt, when our first stop, Port Said, was reached.

We coaled ship here, during which time we viewed this beautiful harbour at the mouth of the Suez Canal. Port Said itself has become a very important trading centre since the Suez Canal was opened. We might perhaps call it the Liverpool of Egypt. The natives are mostly Arabs with a large populace of Jews and Egyptians.

Coaling ship is very dirty work, especially in Port Said and it is amusing, here, to watch the natives at this work. We had only got into the harbour when a sound reached us as if from a host of savages. This sound came from about one hundred coolies who were pulling large lighters with our supply of coal across the harbour. Afterwards I discovered that it was to give the time for all to pull together. While at

The P&O line's *Soudan*, the Hired Transport which carried the Inniskillings to China
Photograph from Album 16, Regimental Museum of the Royal Inniskilling Fusiliers, Enniskillen

Port Said

their task they sing out some favourite tune and by this means they all pull together, just as troops march to time with the band. They transfer the coal from lighter to steamer in containers carried on the shoulder or head. They can coal ship in record time, but they do raise a lot of dust and the ship afterwards had to have a good hosing down.

Suez Canal

We now came to the Suez Canal, which is cut through the Isthmus of Suez and connects Port Said with the town of Suez. This canal has been the greatest undertaking ever accomplished by an engineer. It is about ninety miles long and was cut through a section of the Arabian Desert. Just at the entrance was the statue of the great man whose name has been connected so much with this wonderful canal. His name was Ferdinand de Lesseps and he is of French nationality, but of course we all readily agree, his work was a marvellous feat.

A pilot was taken on board at Port Said to take our ship through the Canal. It runs through two lakes, namely Lake Menzaleh and the Bitter Lake. The north end of the Bitter Lake is where the Israelites were supposed to have crossed when coming out of Egypt, this lake being at that time a portion of the Red Sea. The principal difficulty encountered in the cutting of this canal was the fact that the desert sand formed banks which were constantly slipping in. To remedy this, artificial banks had to be built. The canal is only about 120 feet wide, therefore outgoing vessels are compelled to stop to allow incoming vessels to pass through this narrow passage. The canal is winding in places, so that a steamer at a distance looks as if she was ploughing through the sandy desert. The canal is being widened considerably during the past few years and considerable improvements are being made to facilitate a quicker passage to large steamers. Since the canal was opened in November 1869 it has well repaid for its construction and shares have been very profitable. Although the canal was opened by a French engineer, England has succeeded in holding about eleven twelfths of the shares. In fact England has full command of this canal. She also holds Aden, the key of the Red Sea. From this we see that England has now the key to the Mediterranean at both ends: the Straits of Gibraltar from the West and Aden from the East.

We did not stay there long but proceeded at a monotonous pace along this supernatural stretch of water. It took us a long time to pass through, but we did not mind as we were so near to land that we could see some things of interest which were happening, some in one country on the right and others in another country on the left, or rather two different continents, one side the continent of Africa and on the other side Asia. The railway from Port Said to Cairo runs for a considerable distance alongside the canal. We happened to be the party who had to stop and of course that took up a great deal of time, and as it is so shallow in some parts we had to proceed very cautiously, you may guess what a long time it takes for a vessel to pass through.

The aspect of the desert about Suez is very striking. The whole landscape is like a lightly done piece of toast and the colour of the sea from this contrast looks deeper and brighter. I have mentioned that the ships passing along the course of the canal look as if they were ploughing the desert. When looking north from Suez, it is very striking to see masts of ships in the desert. The water of the canal is not visible from this point and the rigging of a vessel seen moving slowly along has a spectral look about it.

The hot sun acting on the air here has the tendency to make the outlines of the landscape dance and shake and produce the effects of mirage; and one is apt to suppose that a ship seen away over miles of land, under circumstances like these, can only be an optical delusion – an atmospherical effect and not a reality. The term 'ship of the desert' applied to a camel is very expressive and it is generally supposed that the Arab uses these words. It is also supposed that he talks of a ship as the camel of the sea.

In sailing down the Gulf of Suez the land on each side is visible. The burnt-up-looking mountains of the African coast are particularly forbidding in their aspect. On the other side you pass the wells of Moses: the spot can be made out from the few palm trees which owe their existence to the moisture there, and beyond that is all sand. There are mountains in the distance, and as you get south these increase in height.

After dropping the pilot at Suez and leaving the Suez Canal, we pass into the Arabian Sea and from there into the Red Sea, where of course we were able to put on the usual speed. As we passed into the Red Sea, Mount Sinai was clearly pointed out in the distance. This mount is still kept a sacred mount by many pilgrims and the rocks in the valley on either side are covered with numerous characters which are now almost unreadable.

The Red Sea

The Red Sea is never a particularly cool locality, but the month of August is noted as being the hottest in the year, and in our case certainly the heat was terrible, increasing as we went south. There are a few places in the world where the heat is so great that it is said that there is only a sheet of brown paper between them and a certain very hot region. Speaking to one of the ship's crew on this traditional sheet of paper, he replied that during most of the year it was so; but in the month of August the heat was so great that this sheet of brown paper got burnt up and we had not even that protection from the fiery sources of our torment. If you only moved a finger, the perspiration would simply roll off you.

On leaving Suez it was comparatively cool, but even there the vast extent of burning sand we could see gave warning of the sort of ordeal that was before us. As we go on, the desert on each side almost seems flaming. Still, a breeze from the north keeps the ship in a state of tolerable coolness, but there are ominous doubts as to its chances of duration, and when it dies away our real misery is to begin. Sleeping on deck is the fashion, and every night increases the number of what seems like corpses laid out in rows on the poop deck. As we near the Red Sea the ladies find it impossible to exist at night in the cabins and they have their beds brought on deck. Wiping the perspiration from the face and neck is the only possible occupation. If you try to write, great drops gather and come down with a splash as if from a thunder-cloud. Men with bald heads seem to have a crop of pearls always coming up through the skin. All the pores of the body seem like perpetual fountains of water.

The sight on the forecastle is very striking at night. One side is allotted to the Lascars and negroes who do the stoking. The stewards also take refuge here. The remainder is left to the troops and in the evening the whole place gets crowded, every inch of space is covered; the heat is far too great for fun, singing or even conversation; each lays himself down to rest and remains there absorbed with his own sensations until sleep gives him repose. Wherever there is a spot where a man can lay his body it is soon filled. The position of many, nay of nearly all, was that of extreme exhaustion: suggesting with the stillness that it was the sleep of death. They were more like the bodies on a battle field, whose sleep knows no waking. We had the moon with us in the Red Sea, and its light dimly shining through a vapoury sky only helped to make the scene all the more weird-like. On the deck the hammocks are brought up from below and laid down in rows: we all come up in linen knicks: any further covering would be out of the question in such a climate. Where all are so much alike it is difficult to make out your own particular bed: one hears grumbling from some fellow that he can't find his bed, or that it is occupied by somebody else, but quarrelling would be out of the question and soon there is silence all around.

There is another aspect of existence on board ship which ought to be noticed, particularly when we are in the Red Sea: namely, the stokehole. The descent to a stokehole gives one an impression of this section of the ship which will not easily be forgotten. As you descend down the iron ladders, you only escape slipping to the bottom by holding on to a hot iron railing until you reach the Gehenna below, where, stumbling over a lot of coal in the darkness, you find yourself in a region so hot that you could easily suppose that you had just been pitched into one of the furnaces by mistake and that you were a part of the combustion going on by which the steam is produced. A clanking iron door opens and from it comes a glare of light and still more burning heat. With this the living beings of the place become visible, and they are great brawny negroes who come principally from the coast of Zanzibar and whose lot it is to live in this Gehenna of Gehennas. On deck, under an awning, which is watered on the top every hour or so, and with every appliance available, life is still insufferable, and what must it be down here? There are about twelve boilers, six on each side, each with a blazing furnace. Everything around you, even the floor you stand upon, is iron at a burning heat. The poor negroes, accustomed though they may have been to an African sun, often faint at their work down here and have to be carried on deck, where buckets of water are dashed over them till they come back to consciousness.

The cooks on board such a ship are not much better off so far as temperature is concerned; they have to be at work by six in the morning, and before that even, to get the morning cup of tea or coffee ready, and all day they are boiling, baking, roasting and frying till the evening, with a fire on each side of them in the galley. The very slight breeze from the north just moves at about the same speed as the ship and thus the motion of the vessel gives no ventilation: no wind at all would be better. Captains at times stop the engines for a little, to let this slight breath of air blow through and give a little ventilation, and in very hot days they even turn the ship round and sail for a quarter of an hour against the wind.

On leaving the Gulf of Suez and passing through the Straits of Jubal, leaving Shadwan – an island as bare as a biscuit – on the right, land soon disappears on each side. There are islands at times visible on the way down. The first of these are the 'Brothers', two bare rocks just cropping up a few feet above the sea – a most dangerous neighbourhood, for a ship might be on them in a fog with no warning. There is a lighthouse now on one of these. Still farther south is one of the most dangerous places which it is possible to conceive. It is a coral reef extending for some distance. It is nowhere visible; only the surf can be seen and there are only a few feet of water over it. The Arabic name is 'Abdul Kheeson', but our sailors called it the 'Deadleys', a most expressive word in this instance which had its origin, if I am not mistaken, in the loss of *H. M. S. Daedalus* on this reef[6]. There is a lighthouse here now, which, I believe, is kept by four Europeans. Three of them are always in charge and one is away on leave. It must be a curious life in such a place, for there is no dry land: the lighthouse is perched on iron pillars and the waves wash under them. All supplies must be sent from Suez, and that is a two day sail to a steamer.

The next land visible are twelve small islands called the Twelve Apostles. The first island reached is called the island of St. John. What this sunburnt isle has to do with the saint I do not know. Patmos has a valley with one tree in it, called the 'Saint's Garden'. No one could accuse this island of having even a single bush upon it. If St. John ever lived here it would explain why he is always represented with an eagle: it must have been to bring supplies.

There are a good many islands which come into view between here and Perim. Mooshedagerah is the small island on which the *'Alma'* was lost about fifty years ago. On the mainland of Arabia, although not seen from the ship's course, we pass a most important region – that is from a political and religious point of view. It is called the 'Hedjaz', and includes Mecca and Medina, associated with the whole history of Mahomed, and now the place of sacred pilgrimage to all his followers. At Medina is the tomb of the prophet himself. Whoever visits here, at least once in life, acquires a great merit from the journey, a merit giving the performer an extra title of entrance into Paradise.

We now come to Perim, a long low island. There are some buildings around the lighthouse, and a few Seepoys can be made out with a glass in passing. A bazaar, a necessary accompaniment of native Indian troops, can be distinguished, and the British flag may also be seen keeping guard at Bab-el-Mandeb, or the gate of the Red Sea. Bab-el-Mandeb means the Gate of Tears. To us it was the gate of rejoicing (but when we were coming out and not entering the Red Sea). Strong men were looking used up by the heat, weaker men were giving way and many were in hospital. Children, all spotted with prickly heat, cried and knew not what was wrong with them.

As we sailed out by the Gate of Tears, it was almost a perfect calm, not a ripple on the water, only a slight undulation of the surface. This lasted for about a mile or so, when a breath of wind wafted past us, cool and refreshing. This increased to a mild breeze and we felt that it came from quite another source than that which had been scorching us up in the Red Sea. It was in fact a stray puff of the monsoon. Nothing

---

[6] An *H. M. S. Daedalus* was lost in such circumstances on July 2, 1813, but off the coast of Ceylon. A steamship, the *Zealot*, formerly the *Helme Park*, bound for Bombay, struck a coral ridge and sank off this place – 'Daedalus' – in 1887.

could have been more grateful, for all revived under its magic influence. Man, woman and child recovered and soon became like their former selves again.

The political importance of Aden is much greater than the commercial. It is the real key to the Red Sea. Perim is only a sentry box. The straits are about seventeen miles wide and Perim is about two miles from Ras Bab-el-Mandeb, on the Arabian Coast. Batteries can easily command this channel. To command the Red Sea a fleet is necessary, and Aden is its harbour of shelter. What Gibraltar is to the Mediterranean, Aden is to the Red Sea; and by commanding that sea we command the Suez Canal. Whoever holds Aden holds the key of the Suez Canal, and of the commerce between Europe and Asia.

Indian Ocean

The monsoon, in the Arabian Gulf, begins to blow about the end of May or the beginning of June and it lasts until September. It is caused by the flow – as may be called – of the cold air, condensed in the Antarctic Circle, into the regions in which the air is rarefied by the intense heat of India, Arabia and other places. The line of its greatest force is north along the coast of Africa – which tends eastwards to Cape Guardafui. A branch stream of it passes between Cape Guardafui and the island of Socotra, and dies away when it reaches the Arabian coast: but some of it turns west along the Gulf of Aden and it was this sidestream of the monsoon which welcomed us as we left the Red Sea. The monsoon blows, generally speaking, from Africa to Aden as far south as the line[7]. It blows strongest in May or June when it begins, and it carries moisture with it which causes what are called the 'Rains' in India.

The phosphorescence of the Indian Ocean is at times very wonderful. What struck me here, as different from other parts of the sea, was the appearance of bulbs of light, some of them on the surface, bright and flashing; others were more or less deep in the water but still luminous. They suggested the idea that they were stars which had fallen down and been drowned.

Ceylon

Ceylon, with its mountains and well-wooded hills, its fertile green valleys with waterfalls and winding rivers, its ample vegetation and flowers – a spot where all is beautiful – might well have the tradition attached to it that it was the Garden of Paradise. It is still celebrated for its precious stones, although the dealers in these articles are, perhaps,

[7] The Equator.

more famous now-a-days for selling gems whose origin has a closer connection with Birmingham than with Ceylon. In former years Ceylon was better known as the 'Pearliform Island' and the 'Pearl-Drop on the Brow of India'.

For a number of years back the pearl fishing has almost ceased. This has been owing to the destruction of the oysters by a more powerful dweller in these depths, who seems to have a Cleopatra-like taste for dining upon pearls. He has been described as a torpedo fish: but whatever the species, he has a powerful set of instruments, by which he can crush or open the oysters and extract fish, pearls and all. So great have been his ravages that the fishing will not now make any profitable return and it has been all but abandoned.

From a Tamil invasion of Ceylon, there are a number of Hindoos on the island: but the greater number of its people are Buddhists. Tea and coffee planting has so increased during the past years that it overshadows all the other branches of industry, and the coffee and tea plant are now the real pearl of Ceylon and their value is far above that of rubies or sapphires.

Boats in Colombo Harbour

Colombo – the capital – possesses a fine harbour and a breakwater a couple of miles long. The town itself is flourishing in the extreme. Its position in the Indian Ocean makes it a great trading port and steamers bound for the far East and Australia visit its harbour, which makes it a great coaling station. During our stay there we took in a fresh supply of coal and it was amusing to hear the horrible noise the natives made while at their task. Of course it is needless to say what a dirty process is the coaling of a ship: our poor troopship looked a very dejected picture. We were not able to get ashore, but in the distance we could see the extensive tea plantations.

On visiting Colombo for the first time, one will be interested in the strange boats which are peculiar in this part of the world. Seen from some points of view they suggest the idea of a peculiar kind of sea spider, the long pieces of wood projecting into the water having much the appearance of the legs of that description of insect. In constructing their craft, a coco-nut tree forms the keel and at the same time the bottom of the boat. A long and extremely narrow box is built upon it, so narrow that you can merely get your legs in. As such a construction would be certain to turn over, a second piece of cocoa-nut, at the end of two curved branches of a tree, forms a float and a balance. Both boat and counterpoise being so narrow, no resistance is presented to the water, and they go very fast.

The Straits of Malacca

The Straits of Malacca are formed by the Malay peninsula on the east and the island of Sumatra on the west. Singapore is the headquarters of the Straits Settlements. It has a Governor and a very fine Governor's House. Singapore is really a most beautiful spot. The approach from

The coastline of the Straits of Malacca, seen from the Troopship *Soudan*

the sea is very fine. There is a large open bay surrounded by islands of various sizes, all green with foliage from the sea to their highest point. The bay thus protected forms a magnificent harbour. Singapore was not developed as it is today. It was just an island without even a harbour, apart from a landing jetty. The Peninsular and Oriental Company have a wharf in a narrow channel formed by one of these islands. Close to their ground is the residence belonging to the Rajah of Johore; and behind that again is a hill with a flagstaff from whence every ship coming down the straits is seen and signalled.

Singapore, besides Singhalese, contains a very mixed population, among them being a large proportion of Hindoos from the Madras presidency, also a large population of Chinese. The streets of Singapore are all good: so are the roads leading out of the town.

The word Singapore is not Malay, but of Hindostan origin. It means 'Lion's Town' from Singha, a lion. The word Singhalese is from the same root.

Singapore

Around Singapore, the air, the sea and the land are all rich and beautiful in their productions; flowers and fruits are plentiful, for here you are close to the line. Walking sticks seem to be largely cultivated; you cannot move a step without having a bunch of them pressed upon you. You can fit yourself according to taste from the reed-like cane of the sentimental swell to the strong shillelagh-like bludgeon, which would be useful for an Irish fair, or a garrotting attack.

The climate was very hot. We amused ourselves purchasing bananas and throwing coins for the native youths to dive for. The diving boys here are very clever: they surround a vessel as soon as she arrives, and hover around her until she is under way again. Really they seem quite as much at home in the water as if they had been born with fins and scales. When a sixpence is dropped over it never reaches the bottom: the boys tumble in after it and fight and struggle below for the prize – the successful one coming up again to the surface with an air of triumph. They are noisy, amusing rascals, and talk a peculiar kind of broken English. I heard one of them making an appeal, and he tried to explain that the steamer 'now go soon, you no need sixpence any more; throw it down; poor boy dive; suppose you got sixpence in pocket; not good – sixpence make hole in pocket – better throw to poor boy; sixpence good for poor boy. Yes, throw de sixpence; all right, all the boy go down'.

Thus they go on, usually getting a coin, or perhaps a few coppers at last, for they will dive for a penny. After a babyhood and boyhood spent in the water, if they accumulate enough capital, they continue life in the walking stick and bird line.

The China Seas

When leaving Malta for the far East, anxious friends warned me 'to take care of tigers' and 'be careful about snakes', but none of these kind counsellors said a word about mosquitoes or prickly heat. Now, who that has been in India or elsewhere in the East troubles his head on the matter of tigers or snakes? But it is different with the other oriental plagues.

If a man carefully inspects his bed before laying down, it is not the snakes but mosquitoes about which he is anxious. Nearly every bed in the East is covered with a gauze curtain as a defence, and should even one mosquito manage to break this blockade it is a night's rest gone, and the poor suffering wretch is a mass of red swollen spots the next morning. But no defence of this kind prevails against prickly heat, from which, however, some constitutions are exempt. The poor unfortunate who is visited with an attack certainly feels as if clothed with misery. Bright red spots come out all over the body: they are small spots but they increase till the red becomes a bloated mass in places. Job and his comforters is appropriate reading when in this state. You feel as if you had changed clothes with a hedge-hog and put your portion of the costume on outside in. Your mind naturally recalls stories of victims rolled in barrels with nails through the staves. As your misery goes on for days and weeks, you begin at last to think that you have been turned into a pin-cushion as a punishment for your sins. This is the acute form of the disease, which luckily does not always torture to the pitch just described. But at all times there is a wish to use your nails, and if a convenient post should present itself you have constant desire to 'bless the Duke of Argyll'[8]. For about a month I was thus 'blessing' and wishing to die – my comforters consoling me daily with the statement that 'prickly heat is so healthy'.

Two or three days before getting into Hong Kong, we were threatened with a typhoon. To the passengers in general this was not the best of news, but to one with a war map of red spots all over his back a typhoon, a cyclone or a tornado – anything in the shape of cool air – would be welcome. Between Singapore and Hong Kong is the best region for typhoons, and independently of wishes resulting from the prickly heat, I had a desire to see one. Great pains are now taken to get up this sort of thing in theatres, but I prefer at all times to see the real phenomenon, and it was with feelings of hope that I noted the barometer going down. We saw Captain and Officers busy getting ready on board for any emergency. Sails, masts and yards were taken in and everything that could move on deck was made secure: the lore of storms was the subject of conversation; the speed of the engines was reduced, and we cruised about on the watch. Our great object was to find out the direction in which the typhoon moved, so as to be able to dodge it, for the central point of the storm action is very limited; but if you allow the ship to get into its centre, and sail in its course, you may be in it for days; whereas if you see the way it is moving, it can be passed in a very short space of time. No typhoon came, we had very rough weather for two or three days and we got into Hong Kong a day

[8] '. . . The eighth Duke of Argyll, on seeing cattle and sheep being irritated by flies and other beasties dining on their nether regions, erected posts on his estate against which the animals could rub and scratch themselves. This caught the attention of the nation and, whenever Scots would scratch their backs against a post or other object, it became a custom to use the phrase, 'God bless the Duke of Argyll.' From *Clan Campbell Tales* (*http://home.comcast.net/~ccsreg1/index.html*)

after our time. There had been rough weather at Hong Kong, and some slight damage had been done to the shipping.

Typhoon is Chinese, and is formed of *phoon* – wind – and *ty* – storm; from which it will be seen that a typhoon is no particular kind of storm, but only a great wind. The region is very liable to great winds, which do much damage to ships when caught unawares, and a fleet of Chinese junks after one of them is often nothing but a floating mass of ropes, planks and matting. On board our ship there was not much chance of danger of that kind, and I confess to a regret that I had not an opportunity of describing a good typhoon.

We heard that several natives were out with their fishing boats and no doubt by that time many of them were at the bottom of the sea. We saw some of their junks being towed in the next morning and it was a pitiful sight to see the damage that had been done, sails, masts and every loose article blown away and in some cases where a whole family had gone out, only about two or three could be seen to have come back with their boat and sole means of livelihood.

Hong-Kong

The view as you sail into the harbour of Hong Kong is very striking. The steamer, passing round a point, enters a harbour with high hills on the right and houses along the base. We anchored in the harbour for some hours, just sufficient to view this small island with its high peak and houses built right up to the summit. The town of Hong Kong is built up the steep side of the hill and, from the sea, the houses look as if placed on top of each other.

In 1841 Hong Kong was taken possession of in the name of Her Majesty, the spot still being called 'Possession Mount'. Since that date the whole town has come into existence and is named 'Victoria' – Hong Kong, from a 'fragrant harbour', being the name of the island. The Queen's name is most intimately associated with the whole place: the highest point in the island is called 'Victoria Peak', the principal street is called the 'Queen's Road'.

Kowloon, a radius of the mainland opposite Hong-Kong was British Territory. Here was the terminus of the railway connecting Kowloon with Canton. Hong-Kong, a British Colony, appeared to be very loyal to the British throne. The capital named after Queen Victoria has many statues erected in the square both to our former Queen and reigning monarchs succeeding her. A high peak, with Victoria and the harbour at its base, gives one a good view of the mainland beyond. There are many residences and a very fine hotel situated on the top of Victoria Peak. There is also a large hospital to which all invalids are sent in the very warm weather. A tramway system now runs from the town to the top of the peak and it is very

The Hong Kong of almost a century ago, seen from the heights

interesting to watch trams ascend and descend, especially when lying in harbour, as from this point of observation one wonders how trams can run on such an incline. This tramway system is worked by an endless cable with a large engine on the top of the peak by which the cable is carried. Two trams run: as one goes up the other comes down. This arrangement seems dangerous but everything being so well engineered, this tramway has been in existence for years and no accident of any kind has occurred.

A portion of the mainland of China, known as the New Territories, has been ceded to Britain. This, with its high range of hills forms a grand background to Hong Kong and a protection to its harbour. A railway now runs from Kowloon to Canton. So much is European in Hong Kong that it is difficult for a stranger to distinguish what is really Chinese. One ought to wait and see a purely native town before even attempting to judge of what comes before one's eyes. I have heard people talking of India who had only seen Calcutta or Bombay. This is something like judging a house by one of its bricks, and in the case of Calcutta, Bombay and Hong Kong, we can hardly say that the brick belongs to the house. A newcomer into a country can hardly avoid manifesting his ignorance and he is apt to arrive at hasty conclusions. Here I see many who are pure Chinese in features and costume, but their caste or rank I have no power of estimating.

Hong Kong's dramatic tramway

In the harbour we have been surrounded by a large number of the water population, and one cannot help seeing a good deal of their manners and customs. There is constantly a number of boats around the steamer waiting to be employed taking people on shore. The family who own the boat – generally consisting of three generations – all live on board of it, and they all use the oar and help to work the boat. In most cases there is an old woman, evidently the grandmother, and does her work well; then there are babies and children, and the average number on board is four grown-up people and two children. Where they stow themselves away at night is a mystery not yet solved to my own satisfaction, for the space is very confined. There is a loose deck which covers the main sleeping place, at one end of which is the kitchen, and at the other the joss-house or family altar. I persuaded the inmates of one of these boats to lift the hatch, that I might see the altar, and found that it occupied the whole breadth of the boat and about two feet of the length, which is a large expenditure of space, considering the circumstances. There was one principal figure with cups of what seemed oil and water before it, a place for lights, food of various kinds, and plenty of small idols or fancy figures. The family devotions I did not see, for the principal part of the family were hard at work pulling me on shore. I have seen more than one of these families at dinner and was rather astonished at the quantity and apparent quality of food, as well as their power of cooking so much in such a small space. The dishes were all laid out on the hatch or lid over the sleeping place, which formed at the same time both table and seats. I counted five dishes, each containing a different kind of food: in addition there was the great dish of rice, which might be called the *pièce de résistance*, and also a pot with what seemed to be a soup, from which they all helped themselves. All the food seemed not only clean but delicate and savoury. Each dish was composed of more than one material, a fish and a vegetable being cooked together, or some kind of meat and vegetable making a compound.

Every one has a small bowl and a pair of chopsticks, the bowl, filled with rice, being held in the hand; with the chop-sticks he picks up morsels of the delicacies from the platters on the table, and then pushes a lot of rice into his mouth after them. Their cleverness with the chop-sticks is astonishing to a stranger. An Oriental who eats with his fingers cannot manipulate the morsels or convey them to his mouth more dexterously than a Chinaman can with his two slips of wood. An elephant can take up a pin or the heaviest of loads with his trunk, and the chop-sticks have this same variability of power; the smallest particle of food can be picked up and carried from the dish to the mouth, and mountains of rice can be shovelled in. Tit-bits are gathered from the corners of the dish and made into one heap, and the whole is caught up and dipped into any sauce with an ease that no knife and fork could surpass. A man with his bowl held up to about a foot from the head, which is a favourite way of eating, and with the two slender bits of wood in rapid action between the bowl and the mouth, is exactly like a monster insect with its antennae at work. This dexterity is of course the result of a long education, begun very early in life, for we see very small fellows with chop-sticks in their fingers, and no accidents resulting from their use. If there is a baby in the family, it keeps its mouth open, and the mother's chop-sticks act for it till it is able to use a pair for itself.

Hong Kong Chinese, chopsticks in evidence

In the East, the use of the fingers for conveying food to the mouth is the universal rule. In India, from a coolie to a Maharajah, from a Sudra to a Brahmin, the use of a knife, a fork, or a spoon to eat with is altogether unknown. The chop-stick is a development beyond this, and is common to the whole of China, Mongolia, and Japan – a vast mass of people. On the western side of the Himalayas chop-sticks or any such aids to eating are entirely unknown. There is something very peculiar in this marked distinction in habits of two races. I have no doubt but there is an ethnic meaning underlying this difference, and its study might help to throw light on the origin of the race.

After leaving Hong-Kong we find the coast fringed with a multitude of islands of various sizes. Some are mere rocks of a few yards in extent, others are large and cultivated. Fleets of fishing boats may be seen busy at work, and junks of all kinds are constantly knocking about.

Tales of rough weather during the north-east monsoon are recounted on board ship, and the place where such and such a ship was lost is pointed out as we go along. Such tales are not very cheering to a timid landsman; the supposition comes naturally into his mind that we might all be thrown on one of those desolate rocks before tomorrow morning, and he frames a question or two accordingly. The inquiry no doubt will be as to the character of the natives and the chances of the ship-wrecked who fall into their hands. 'All pirates, Sir' is the answer; and the fate of ships and their crews becomes a new theme for yarns, which do not tend to soothe the feelings of the nervous.

The China Coast

The China coast is pested with pirates, who either dwell along the coast or seek refuge on the small islands. This unwelcome population have been wreckers and pirates for ages, and have never known any

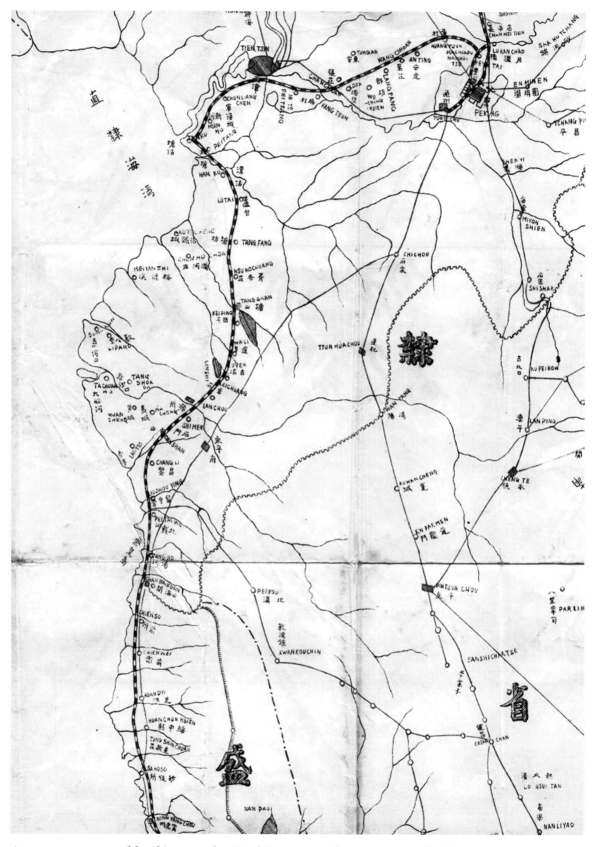

A contemporary map of the China coast that Hutchinson came to know. Tientsin and Peking inland, top; Shan-Hai-Kwan below, on the Imperial Railway, with a crenellation sign for the Great Wall, starting out from the Yellow Sea.

better ideas of making a livelihood than that of plunder. Within the last few years a good deal has been done to put down piracy, and so far matters are improved. The various powers have small gunboats all along the coast; and should any vessel get wrecked and her crew be ill-treated, so soon as the news gets to Hong Kong, Shang-hai or Wei-Hai-Wei[9], the island is made for, and the assailants captured under these circumstances seldom escape death. As these pirates have lately had more than one dose of this kind, they are now more careful in their treatment of European ships. Still, small steamers plying between Tientsin and Hong Kong are very often boarded at night, and plundered. Their plan with a European ship is to kill all the crew, as dead dogs tell no tales; then, after taking whatever they want from the vessel they set her on fire or scuttle her. With native junks their plan is different. They seldom touch a European ship now, unless she becomes a wreck; but with junks they are not so particular, for Chinamen do not seem to have any energy for self-defence. This seems strange under such circumstances, for they know the certain fate which awaits them. The captured junk is taken to the pirates' village, the property on board is divided, and the craft is broken up for firewood. The crew are not maltreated, for they never show any resistance; they are divided among the principal men of the gang, and are kept as slaves to work and do the most menial of duties. Should any gunboat visit that place – and the Chinese Government have now some small craft for cruising about these islands and looking after pirates – these unfortunates are concealed in underground places made for the purpose. A number of men are placed beside them, with large knives, and should any of them attempt to shout, so as to call the attention of the people searching the village, they are instantly cut to pieces. These prisoners have almost no chance of escape, and slavery for life is their doom.

On the Admiralty charts for this coast the word 'Piratical' is added in an underline to the name of many of the islands. This tells of the past and, indeed, of the present also, but it is a condition of things the days of which are numbered.

The Yellow Sea is clearly named from its colour. There need be no uncertainty on this point, as in the case of the Red Sea. The Yang-Tse-Kiang, and Huang-Ho, or Yellow River, send down such large volumes of turbid water that the sea is yellow for many miles, and beyond that a yellowish grey extends far into the ocean, till at last it is lost in the pure waters of the deep. From the contrast of the yellow with the dark blue beyond it, they call the latter the 'Black Sea'. The yellow is the yellow of ochre, indicating that the rivers have passed through a soil of ferruginous earth. The water seems thick with the yellow matter in it;

[9] Wei-Hai-Wei was a territory in Shantung leased by Britain in 1898 and returned to China in 1930: see Chapter 7.

The railhead at Ch'in-Huang-Dao

so much so is this the case that a Yankee is reported to have said, 'Call that water? Why, it's more like what we make bricks with in our parts'. After sailing for a day or two on yellow water, I more fully appreciated that provision of nature which has made the whole ocean blue. Had waters been all yellow, like the Yellow Sea, it would have been a very dull monotonous affair. Yachting and sea-bathing would have been out of the question. The fish found in such waters are said to be poor and tasteless; but it is easy to believe that it is the natural element of junks and Chinamen. In looking over the Yellow Sea which extended in every direction to the horizon, it had much the appearance of a desert of sand, suggesting a great liquid Sahara; and had one been a tired traveller, it would have betokened nothing more drinkable to the thirsty throat than that weary plain.

When about a day's sail from Ch'in-Huang-Dao – our port of landing – we passed close to Port Arthur[10], the key of the recent Russia-Japanese war. The hills surrounding the harbour are dotted with monuments, I suppose to many brave soldiers who fell on this memorable day. We could discern many trenches and parapets which were used during the war, and which have since remained untouched.

On 2nd November 1909, experiencing a taste of rough sea and pitching and tossing on the waves, we sailed into the port of Ch'in-Huang-Dao, in the Gulf of Pei-chi-li, where our voyage on the *H. T. Soudan* had come to an end. This port is merely a promontory jutting into the sea. As a branch line from the main Imperial Railway runs out along this, it is very convenient for transferring freight. The steamer anchored alongside the long pier, where the train that was to take us on to Tientsin awaited us. Ch'in-Huang-Dao is a splendid place for dis-embarkation and a great deal of labour was dispensed with. The ship's cranes just lifted the baggage out of the holds and placed it in the awaiting luggage vans and we were soon steaming and puffing along to our final destination.

[10] Port Arthur is nowadays known as Lueshun, in Liaoning Province.

2 The Battalion in north China

IT was at Ch'in-Huang-Dao that we first experienced the extreme cold of North China. This was a vast change and perhaps a quick one for it was only a few weeks ago since we were almost scorched up in the Red Sea. Not only was the Red Sea a warm locality, for our voyage to Hong-Kong was in no sense cool. Hong-Kong has a very warm climate all the year round. When passing through Hong-Kong, bathing was the fashion. After leaving Hong-Kong the climate got cooler as we sailed north to Ch'in-Huang-Dao where the extreme cold took great effect. We had often heard that we would experience extreme cold in this part of the Far East and it is only true we found it so. What an awful train journey that was: although we had our greatcoats on, still the cold penetrated through to our bodies.

We entrained at Ch'in-Huang-Dao for Tientsin and travelled by the Imperial Railway. This is the longest railway in North China. It has its terminus at Peking and runs through to Moukden via Tientsin where it is connected up with the Trans-Siberian Railway. It was a 10 hours run to Tientsin, a distance of about 180 miles. As we journeyed along, our attention was focused on the strange appearance of this Celestial Empire and its curious population. We had not gone far on our journey until I noticed something about this country which made it differ very much from my own. 'We have not crossed a road yet' was the remark from one. 'No, nor I don't think you will' was the reply from another, for China is not possessed of such luxuries. There are no roads in China, just cross country tracks. The absence of roads makes a country look neglected, and wanting of something. The Chinese think

One of the largest bridges on the Imperial Railway. (See also photograph on page 125).

more of preserving the graves of their forefathers than the making of macadamised roads, for the whole country looks like a vast burial ground. The graves, too, are curious in their aspect: they look more like large mounds of earth. The railway on which we travelled looked very bare and wanting of something also. It was the fencing on each side that was missing. The railways run through open country without any protection whatever. The animals in those parts being as much frightened of the 'foreigner's' invention as the natives themselves, accounts I think for the absence of fences.

On our way up we passed T'angshan coal mines and works. There are fine works here and the coal mines being so convenient makes it even more important. It is better known by British residents of these parts as the Birmingham of China. The Railway works are also situated here, which made me christen it in my own mind the 'Inchicore' of the Imperial Railway. There is a splendid steel bridge here also, perhaps a piece of the engineering from these works.

A shorter and perhaps more interesting way of reaching Tientsin is by the Pei-Ho river[11], and travellers usually select this route. In this case it was impossible, for the *H. T. Soudan* could never navigate the shallow and winding Pei-Ho, but smaller steamers can get up with a little difficulty. The nearest port, Tientsin, is about fifty miles from its mouth. I have reached Tientsin by both routes and found that the Pei-Ho route was very much shorter. On entering the Pei-Ho river one gets a good view of the old Taku Forts which were almost completely demolished during the Boxer troubles of 1900. The river itself is celebrated for its 'bends'. It curves in and out like a snake. Many of the bends are so angular that steamers have to run their bow into a cabbage garden, and a hawser has to be carried out and made fast on the other side before the place can be passed. This makes the navigation of the Pei-Ho slow, and gives an anxious time to the captain. His last great difficulty is the 'Everlasting Bend' and then it is pretty plain sailing up to Tientsin.

At Taku the country is open and flat: and what strikes one is that, as far as the eye can see, there is a crop of ancestral graves. They are circular mounds like moleheaps, and are so thick and close that the whole country has the appearance of being one vast burial ground. They recalled to me the saying of the Arabs, that, when a man dies, 'he has gone to the greater number'.

The banks of the Pei-Ho are dotted with little cities and villages. The walls of the houses are made of sun-dried bricks and their low slanting roofs are made of bundles of reeds plastered with mud. The houses are all built of one storey and, indeed, they look more like boxes than houses for some of them are not more than fifteen feet square. They

---

[11]   The Pei-Ho river is nowadays referred to as the Hai-Ho (Haihe).

Ancestral graves

are built close to the streets, which are narrow dirt roads without sidewalks. In some places parts of the buildings extend out over the banks of the river, and the freshets often wash the foundations away, and drop such houses, families and all, into the water. Another disagreeable time of the year is the rainy season which is in process from the middle of July to the middle of August, although some years it is longer. I have seen thousands of acres of cultivated and other land completely under water, and vast numbers of the poor class of Chinese completely washed away. Of course it would be no protection for them to get on the roofs, because the roofs would not bear the strain and would collapse.

When sailing up the river one sees both in front and behind the queer sails of Chinese boats, apparently floating through the green fields as they pass along the course of the river. The great quantity of sand brought down by the river gives it a dirty yellow appearance and the sediment which gathers tends to make the river very shallow, thereby obstructing the passage of steamers. To remedy this, dredging operations have to be continually carried on. Engineering experts are engaged in grappling with the problem of obtaining a navigable channel through the Taku Bar, so that vessels of 14 or 15 feet draught may pass without hindrance.

On arrival at Tientsin we were welcomed by many of the foreign population from the Concessions, including troops of the various nationalities stationed here. After leaving the station we marched over the International Bridge through the French and British Concessions, thence to the British Barracks. This barracks is rectangular in shape and divided by a wall and passage. We occupied one half while the Punjabis occupied the other. The barrack compound also had a hospital and detention barracks. The Military Hospital was situated just outside the compound. The married quarters were two-storeyed buildings along both sides of the road leading to the barracks entrance.

A dredger at work on the Pei-ho

Our quarters were single-storeyed brick buildings. Each room, besides the normal furniture, was equipped with a large boiler-shaped stove in the centre from which a steel pipe projected through the roof: a reminder of the cold winters here. Coal was plentiful and these stoves could eat it up. The drawback however was that the room was alternatively warm and cold, depending on the fuel in the stove. We had an issue of winter clothing shortly after arrival, including fur coats, lug caps and gloves. Before our first winter expired we felt the need for these.

The climate of Tientsin, like that of all North China is fine or fearful, according to the way one looks at it. The occasional dust storms in Spring and Autumn are certainly disagreeable, as is also the short rainy season from the middle of July to the middle of August. But the beautiful succession of bright sunshiny days of Winter are a joy that one fails to remember only during the long hot days of midsummer. The thermometer travels from about zero (32 degrees of frost) in January, when the rivers in N. China are frozen over to a depth of about 18 inches, to 105 or 110 degrees in June or early July. It is an open question which of these extremes is more beneficial to the foreigner's health. Later in July and in August the presence of moisture in the air brings the temperature down to about 75 or 85 degrees. It is during this period that the mosquitoes are most tormenting. These little insects infest every nook and corner and without mosquito curtains a peaceful sleep would be out of question.

About 200 of our regiment, one Company, in addition to a mounted infantry (mule) corps, went on to be stationed in the Legation at Peking. Whether at Peking or Tientsin the set-up was international. Since the Boxer Rising in 1900, when foreigners were murdered without mercy, foreign governments have stationed troops in China to guard their respective nationals there. Tientsin may be divided into two sections, i.e. the native city and the foreign Concessions. In Peking the foreigners' quarters are known as Legations. As to the population of Tientsin, the figures of the foreign settlements are British 600, Germans 500, Japanese 1,984, French 250, American 150, Russian 50, Austrian 45, Belgians 25 and others 200. Making a total of foreign population of about 3,800: this is of course exclusive of the military.

Duties were light apart from a few guards and the usual parades and route marches.

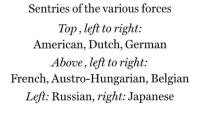

Sentries of the various forces
Top, left to right:
American, Dutch, German
Above, left to right:
French, Austro-Hungarian, Belgian
Left: Russian, *right:* Japanese

Sports

Sport was plentiful. In winter, skating and ice hockey were healthy pastimes. Football, tug-o-war and other sports, with the various foreign troops, were very popular. We were however at a loss for a suitable building or gymnasium for use as a concert hall: with such a building the married families could have been better catered for. In spite of this Company concerts were held in the appropriate dining rooms, and were usually appreciated.

The marquee at the Regimental Sports Day of the 27th Inniskillings, Tientsin

It was on 10th May 1910 that our first sporting test came. The French had their annual International Sports on that date. We trained a tug-o-war team and mustered other eligible competitors to take part in the various events, including the 26 miles marathon race, a speciality event with the French. Only a limited number of N.C.Os and men, for obvious reasons, were permitted to attend these sports.

The French Barracks were situated some three miles outside the Russian Concession. Some went by transport while others hired rickshaws. The first event was the marathon race, which started across country very early on that morning. We had a few competitors for that: by the time the sports proper had commenced, these runners were reported to be nearing the finishing line in the sports field. To our delight it was announced that one of our competitors, Private Duffy, was leading. He just finished a short distance in front of a Frenchman. He was justly proud in his achievement. As the French had always won this event it was a proud day for us that an Inniskilling had beaten them for the first time. One of our men paced him home on a cycle in the last few hundred yards. In the long jump, Sgt. F. Gorman got second prize. Sgts. Gorman and Modler won prizes in the long and high jumps. Many of the other events such as the pole jump, throwing the shot etc went to the French.

A tug-of war contest

Our chief interest now was the tug-o-war, having beaten our competitors and getting into the semi-final against the French who had not yet been beaten in this event in China. According to French rules, there was no limit as to weight and the pull was 'last man over'. Under such rules our men, though tough and strong, could in no manner come up to the weight of such big men as the French team were. It was a long and desperate pull but in the end the weight won.

The following year we again trained a team and, being determined to win next time, our team was put on special training coupled with a special diet for months before the event. This time, although the pull was desperate, our team beat them for the first time in their history. When the day came, our team once more met the French. And what a pull. Our team from sheer training held that rope for 20 minutes at least. The French had the weight but they failed to hold on for such a period and finally had to let go. It was guts and determination gave us the victory: the French were amazed and disappointed.

On the evening of the French Sports, 10th May 1910, as we were about to return to our Barracks, a message came through that our King, H.M. King Edward VII, had passed away. All cheering and rejoicing ceased, and we returned to Barracks quietly.

A terrible bubonic plague in 1910 killed at least one million Chinese. Few if any foreigners were infected. We were inoculated and prohibited from visiting Chinese locations as a precaution.

On St. Patrick's Day 1910 the Battalion, under the command of Lt. Col. C. J. L. Davidson D.S.O. carried out the ceremony of

A disinfection unit

Trooping the Colour, the Brigadier taking the salute at the 'March Past'.

The recreation ground adjoining the Concession was the venue, the 'Square' being manned by the Punjabi Regiment, who with us formed the Brigade in Tientsin. Our spectators on this occasion were very cosmopolitan. Coming from the various Concessions, the wives and families belonging to the Regiment were also present in force. The Colours were carried by Lieutenants Kirkpatrick and Sullivan, with Colour Sergeant D. Connor as escort.

景光之祭旗軍軍屯駐國英日七十月三年一十百九千
Trooping, the Colors I.R. Inniskilling in Tientsin, 17, mar 1911

One problem in Tientsin was to know the correct time. To overcome this a time gun was fired each day at noon, to which clocks were timed.

Chinese labour was employed for many of the menial duties in Barracks, especially in the cook house, for washing up &c. Chinese have a craze for pilfering and many of them were caught carrying off meat and other food. The punishment for this offence was usually flogging. Sergeant Gallagher in charge of the Detention Barracks invariably carried out such punishment. For fear of retaliation from the Chinese outside, he seldom left the barracks.

Although the Inniskillings fraternised with most of the other foreign contingents, we noticed that the French and Germans were not so inclined towards each other. While the French were always anxious for our comradeship, the Germans were even more so. Officers and N.C.Os frequently visited our respective Officers' and Sergeants' Messes. It was usually arranged that only members of the same nationality would visit at the one time, just in case of any unpleasant incidents. Were it not for the language problem, we could have had a more pleasant time with these foreign troops.

An unusual route march

We usually did one route march each week. On one occasion we set off as usual, our destination, unknown to the ranks at least, being the French Barracks about four miles from the Concessions. We marched on to the French parade ground where the French troops were already lined up in column. We then marched past the French troops with their O.C. in command, our O.C. giving the salute and 'Eyes Left'. We then formed up in close formation when the French troops, forming up in quarter column, marched past in a similar salute. The salutes being over, both parties piled arms and were dismissed for half an hour to mingle together and fraternise with each other. We had a few men who knew some French and they were in great demand, the Frenchmen flocking around them. Most of the conversations, however, were in 'Pidgin English' as used mostly in Tientsin.

It was some time before we got our battalion together again, some having visited the French quarters and wining rather well, for the French are very hospitable. This ceremony of course was previously arranged between our C.O. and the French C.O. It certainly did a lot to increase the friendship between both units.

The sincerity of the friendship built up with the German contingent during our period in Tientsin resulted in a very unusual incident which occurred eight years later in France during the 1914–18 war. Our battalion one night took over a front line trench. The enemy facing them on that night was none other than their former friends in Tientsin. How those Germans knew that the Inniskillings were there is still a mystery. Messages were signalled across No

French troops parade their colours in Tientsin

A shave from the Indian barbers

Man's Land and during that night both parties visited each other's trenches. Needless to say, not a shot was exchanged during that night.

It was in Tientsin that the troops had their first experience of the Indian barber. In India the native barber was commonplace. In Tientsin also Indians were employed. As one barber is allotted to each Company, it is essential that he commences his shaving shortly after 'Lights Out' in order to have all the Company shaved before first parade. It is an experience to be shaved while asleep, for the Indian barber will shave you whether awake or not. He passed along from cot to cot, his stock-in-trade consisting of a small lamp, a shaving brush, tin of lather and a breast pocket of cut-throat razors. Should one not be awake, well, he shaved him while he slept.

Sandstorms can be severe in North China. We were caught in one while on a route march and had difficulty in getting back to Barracks. When Tommy Atkins looks at himself in a looking-glass and sees how dirty his face is after struggling through one of these storms, he is not long in coming to the conclusion that a good supply of soap and water is necessary. You would hardly believe what a hard task it is to remove that dust, especially so around the eyes. I have heard it said that these dust storms are the cause of the Chinese having such small eyes, owing to keeping them almost closed on account of so much dust flying about: whether it is true or not I cannot really say, but it appears probable.

3 *Tientsin*

Tientsin may be divided in two sections, viz. the Native City and the foreign Concessions.

The Concessions

The foreign Concessions in Tientsin are situated south-east of the city, along the banks of the Pei-Ho river. The Japanese, French, British and German on the west bank, and the Italian, Russian and Belgian on the east[12]. Although Tientsin is the name given to the foreign Concessions – while the native quarter is known by distinction as Tientsin City – the name of Tientsin really belongs to the native city only. The Chinese name of the foreign Concessions is Sze-Chu-Lin, this being the name of a Chinese village originally situated in the mud flats and swamps from which the foreign town has arisen. Some natives live in the Concessions but usually they either work for, or do business with, the foreigners. The water supply of the foreign concessions is obtained from the river and is passed through the filter beds of one or other of the two water-works companies, the Tientsin Water-works Company Ltd. and the Tientsin Native City Water-works Company Ltd. The water is quite safe and wholesome to drink and no outbreak of disease was ever attributed to this source.

A visit to the foreign Concessions gives one an impression such as is gained at a cinematograph theatre, where panoramic views of various European cities are being illustrated, the sudden change from one Concession to another giving a similar effect. You can judge for yourself what a magnificent town has sprung up from a small village.

The Concessions are modifications of the countries they represent. As we come into the German Concession (see coloured slide in centre-spread), we find German architecture prevailing, streets with German names, and even the Chinese coolies trying to speak German. The buildings of this Concession with few exceptions are all residential. The principal street is Wilhelm Strasse. A fine old building, which was erected by the late Viceroy Li-Hung-Chang and known as the Imperial University, has now been acquired by the German Government and converted into a barracks for the German troops. At the far end of the main thoroughfare, a handsome statue of the Old German

---

[12] Hutchinson here omitted to mention the Austro-Hungarian legation, which was also on the east bank.

hero 'Roland' has been erected in memory of the German soldiers who fell in the Boxer troubles of 1900, and around its base are recorded the different actions and expeditions in which the German troops took part. The Tientsin Rowing Club have their boat-house in this concession and it is situated in a very picturesque spot.

The statue of Roland, commemorating the German dead of the Boxer Rebellion

A continuation of Wilhelm Strasse brings us into the British Concession. This is the most important of all the Concessions, as it contains the principal *hongs*, banks and stores. The most important building is the Gordon Hall – situated in the Victoria Road which is the main thoroughfare – it is named after that grand old man General Gordon[13], who at the time of the Taiping rebellion[14] drew up the plans for the construction of this Concession. In this building are situated the Municipal Council Rooms with the foreign and Chinese staff, the Municipal Library, which numbers 8,000 volumes and subscribes to 24 periodicals, and a large entertainment hall with a well-equipped stage. In the main audience room can be seen numerous memorial tablets to the soldiers and sailors of the different nations who died in the Siege of Tientsin in 1900. I might also say here that it was in this building that a few of the Inniskillings resided during the time of the late revolution.

The prettiest spot in the British concession is the Victoria Park adjoining the Gordon Hall. In the centre is an ornamental band

Corporal James Hutchinson (right) and a comrade Lance-Corporal

[13] Major-General Charles George Gordon, CB 1833–1885, known as 'Chinese Gordon' and, later, 'Gordon of Khartoum'.

[14] This 13-year rebellion, effectively a civil war from 1851 to 1864, had pitted anti-Manchu and anti-establishment discontents against the Qing administration. The latter prevailed in the end with assistance from Britain and France, but not before many millions of Chinese were killed.

stand[15], and during the summer months the bands of the different military contingents give open air performances (see centre-spread) which attract crowds from all quarters of the city. The park on these occasions presents a very animated scene: the aristocracy of Tientsin, nurse-maids, Chinese in their gaudiest attire and last but not least the soldiers from the different Concessions with their mixture of uniform.

In the south-east corner of the park stands a very large bell mounted on a concrete basement. The outside of the bell is covered with numerous Chinese characters. This large bell formerly hung for many years in the old 'Treaty Temple' – now converted into a barracks for the Japanese troops. The characters round the bell show that it was presented to Li-Hung-Chang by the Krupp Iron Works[16]. After the troubles of 1900, this large bell was handed over to the British Municipal Council and is now used as a fire alarm bell: the tolling of it can be heard a considerable distance away.

The Astor House, the largest hotel in Tientsin, stands opposite the Victoria Gardens. This hotel is a favourite residence for travellers visiting Tientsin. Our attention is now drawn to the Tientsin Club, a large and magnificent building in close proximity to the Astor House. Although it is a British club it has members of all nationalities and visitors to the port are permitted to make use of it for a certain time on

The bell presented to Viceroy Li-Hung-Chang by the Krupp Iron Works

[15] By the 1980s, a Chinese-style pavilion had been built on the stone base of the bandstand.

[16] The first contacts between Krupp and China had been in 1866: the firm began to supply China with munitions in the 1870s.

being introduced by a member. All the business houses of the British Concession are situated in Victoria Road, while nearly all the private residents are situated in Meadows Road. Here are the private quarters of most of the British officers. We are also shown the Old Club Room which was used by the Tientsin Volunteer Corps. It contains a proper gymnastics space, a boxing ring and in a separate room stand several rows of firearms belonging to the Corps. The old club was used for concerts and dances as well as being a drill hall for the volunteers and during the Revolution of 1912, a party of the Inniskillings used it as a barracks.

Entering Meadows Road we see the buildings of the English Chinese Engineering and Mining Company and then there comes into view the spire of a fashionable little church which was called All Saints Church, its denomination being Church of England. At the entrance of the building next to the church we see a flagstaff from which flutters the dear old Union Jack and this we are told is the residence of the General Officer Commanding troops in North China. There marching up and down, his bayonet glittering in the sun, is a British sentry on duty at the gate entrance, one of our comrades of the old 27th.

We then pay a visit to the Recreation Ground where we see a splendid rugby ground and also a space for the Association Football game, where many a hard battle has been decided. There is no mistake, it is kept in a splendid condition. Opposite the Recreation Ground stands the Union Church – Congregationalist – in Park Road. The latter is a quaint little building which reminds me of the little country church at home[17].

Next we come to our own barracks, one of the dull portions of the concession. I have heard it said that at one time it was a Chinese village but I would not like to say whether it was true or not: I am rather inclined to disbelieve it. I might just say this, that the last time I saw the barracks there had been vast improvements made: at the entrance a large clock had been put up and the interior had been ornamented by rows of young trees. The British barracks are situated in Bristow Road, a considerable distance outside the Concession. The barracks are divided into two sections: one section is allotted to the British troops while the other accommodates the British Indian troops.

A continuation of the Victoria Road brings us to the French Concession. This Concession is much smaller than the British, but contains some fine French business houses, the majority of the Mission Headquarters, the Chinese Post Office, St. Louis Roman

[17] Hutchinson was probably referring here to St John The Baptist Church in his birthplace, Coolbanagher. It has the distinction of being the only church designed – in 1790 – by the famous Georgian architect, James Gandon. It was erected by the Earls of Portarlington, of Emo Court nearby, where Hutchinson's mother is known to have worked. Related Hutchinsons have lived in Coolbanagher from at least the 18th century and still do so today.

Catholic Church with its spires, a Y.M.C.A. and the Arcade, a theatre on a small scale and the only place of amusement in the foreign section of Tientsin. One of the largest buildings in this concession is the Imperial Hotel, which is supposed to be the second best in Tientsin. There is also a Chinese market place where anything and everything can be purchased at a very cheap rate. I saw a very large fish measuring about 3 feet sold for 30 cents, or 6d. in English money. I wondered to myself what a fishmonger's price at home would be. Everything seemed to be the same: a bunch of grapes could be purchased for 10 cents, 2d. in English money. In the hardware line everything appeared remarkably cheap.

The Japanese Concession adjoins the French. Here the growth has far outrun that in any of the other Concessions. Indeed Japan-in-Tientsin has had the largest growth in trade, in population and in building. In this Concession stands the old Treaty Temple[18] – now the Japanese military barracks. In the Japanese park[19] stands a memorial, erected to the memory of the Japanese soldiers who fell in the siege of Tientsin in 1900. It is a tall rough slab of stone, perhaps the most artistic of its kind, and is commonly known as the 'Broken Column' (see centre-spread). In this park also stands a monument to the memory of the American Colonel Emerson H. Liscum, who was killed on the spot where the monument now stands, during the advance on Tientsin City in 1900[20]. The monument is a small obelisk and is situated inside the Japanese Recreation Ground.

An electric tramway built by a Belgian company runs from the Chinese City through the Japanese and French Concessions, across the International Bridge to the entrance of the railway station. The charge for that long journey was 3 cents or three-fifths of a penny. The International Bridge[21], which spans the Pei-Ho river, joins the French with the Russian Concession. An enormous amount of traffic is continually moving to and fro across this bridge, including foreigners of all nationalities, Chinese with their curious vehicles, including the rickshaw – the most common conveyance in these parts. The traffic is very often delayed as the bridge has to be opened to allow the boats on the river to pass through, therefore carriages, rickshaws, trams and pedestrians are at a standstill.

[18] Known in Chinese as the Hai-Guang-Ssu: treaties were negotiated here between China and the Western powers in 1858.

[19] The Japanese name of this park, established in 1907, is Yamato Koen.

[20] The assault to recover Tientsin from the Boxers had begun on 13 July 1900. At approximately 0900 hours the Colour Sergeant of the US Infantry was severely wounded. Colonel Emerson Hamilton Liscum had been struck in the shoulder but gallantly seized the Colours from the fallen sergeant, stood fearlessly holding them erect and continued to direct the assault on the city walls in the face of murderous fire. A few moments later, the Colonel fell mortally wounded and shortly after directing his men to 'Keep Up The Fire, Men' he died.

[21] Today called the Liberation Bridge.

The Russian is the largest of all the Concessions. Here we see numerous hotels, cinematograph halls and some fine looking shops. Turning off the main road and proceeding along the bank of the river we come to one of the prettiest spots in all Tientsin in the shape of a small green coppice, planted thickly with trees, which makes it delightfully cool in summer. It stands out quite prominent on account of its dull surroundings. In the centre is a handsome monument with its shining cupola which dazzles the eyes when the sun is out and makes it visible from a considerable distance. This monument was erected to the memory of the Russian soldiers who fell during the troubles of 1900. Around the monument are placed several old guns which were captured from the Chinese. We wend our way back and find ourselves at the Railway Station, which is situated at the very end of the Russian Concession.

The monument to the Russian troops killed in 1900

The Native City

Many foreigners living in the Concessions never have occasion to go to the Native City and therefore are not aware of what an interesting place it is. As we had heard about it we took a stroll in that direction and on our tour through it came to the conclusion that it was one of the most interesting places we had yet seen. The curiosity shops alone were the means of passing away a couple of hours and curios could be bought dirt cheap. Then there were the shops where costumes were sold and, no mistake, there were garments which at home would raise a good price and could be had in the city for from 10 to 40 dollars: no doubt some of these robes of Princes and Generals would fetch about £50 to £100 at home. At last we left the City and its wonderful attractions and were pleased that we did not shun it, like a good many residents. We were told of one of the early residents who had lived in Tientsin for forty years and had only visited the Native City twice.

In speaking of Chinese cities generally it may be said that there is no outward grandeur in any of the buildings. The houses, frequently combining both shop and dwelling house, are usually of one storey, never more than two. Even if there were grand, tall structures, such as we see in India, in these Chinese cities, so narrow are the streets and so crowded the houses that nothing could be seen to advantage.

There are no prominent buildings, with the exception of the pawnbrokers' towers; even many of the temples are low, scarcely arising above the surrounding houses, and altogether the view from without has nothing that is striking or interesting.

The throng of Tientsin's Native City

The streets, though narrow and irregular, supply an endless variety of interesting pictures. The main streets are fairly wide, but the side streets are never more than 8 or 10 feet wide: they will not admit the passage of any wheeled carriage, the only mode of conveyance for passengers being the sedan-chair, which is suspended on poles and carried on the shoulders of coolies. Merchandise is often carried in the same way in the towns, but in the country pack horses and wheel-barrows are also used. Some of the streets are perfect bazaars, the shops on either side being filled with costly articles, well arranged for effect, rich jewellery, silks of all kinds, curiosities of every description, and all sorts of ornamental and fancy work.

The principal streets are hung with gay banners suspended from the tops of the houses and from the fronts of the shops. The brightly coloured signs give a showy appearance to the fronts of the buildings. The Chinese are very clever in the getting up of advertisements: they believe in 'pushing' business and consequently have some very 'catchy' means of advertising their goods. The advertisement which struck me most was the 'clock face': at first sight, I thought it was the sign of a watchmaker's shop but afterwards discovered that it hung over the drapery as well as the curio store. It is merely the sign that the shop is up to time with its goods and prices.

The great variety of curious articles exposed to public view by the open doors, the noisy tide of human beings which is all the while surging through these narrow avenues, the processions which one often meets and which take up the whole street as they pass along, make up such a scene as is not to be found in any other part of the world.

Every city in China is surrounded by a high brick wall. Tientsin is now an exception to this, for after the Boxer troubles of 1900, the foreigners tore down the city wall, when many of the bricks were sent to Wei-Hai-Wei for use in building there. Around the city where the walls used to stand is a wide macadamised street called Ma-Lu[22] or Horse Street. But now even the horse has been superseded by electricity, and there are eight miles of tramway in operation. Tientsin claims the honour of having the first tram line in China. The principal streets are now lighted by electricity. Steam rollers and sprinklers for the streets, an efficient health department, telegraph, telephone and fire stations are some of the modern improvements.

Whenever a house or shop is burned, or falls to decay, a slice of a few feet from the property is annexed to the street before a permit for re-building is issued. In this way the main streets of the city are being gradually widened.

The original city of Tientsin has been a place of commercial importance for many years. To Tientsin came several highways from different directions. As it was a port of the northern sea, the head of the Grand Canal and the Gateway of the Capital, a large part of the tribute rice from the entire Empire passed through its waterways. The principal waterways of Tientsin are the Pei-Ho, the Hai-Ho, the Grand Canal and the Lu-tai Canal. The Hai-Ho joins the Pei-Ho at Tientsin. The Grand Canal is merely a tributary of the Pei-Ho which flows down from Peking.

The enormous amount of traffic centering in these waterways contributes largely to the importance of the city. This with the railway facilities so rapidly developing already makes it a distributing point for four provinces, besides Manchuria and Mongolia. Even from Tibet come contributions to Tientsin's trade in the shape of wool, sometimes taking twelve or fourteen months to reach here. During the winter months when the rivers are frozen, Tientsin trades through the ice-free port Ch'in-Huang-Dao.

Tientsin, being the official residence of the Viceroy of the Province[23], adds greatly to its political importance. Perhaps the reform which is most far-reaching in its effects, and strikes deepest at the root of Chinese conservatism, is in the matter of education. Discontinuing the old examination system and turning the temples into schools throughout the Empire is a more important step and a more radical one than friends of China could have dreamed of fifteen years ago. And yet this conversion of temples is rapidly going on. Especially is it noticeable here in Tientsin. Of the more than thirty former temples, seven are now turned over entirely to school purposes, five are official headquarters of some kind, three are occupied as charity institutions, while in others the main part is used as a school and a small part reserved for temple worship. What is done with all the

[22]   Still so known today.
[23]   This Province was known at the time as Chihli.

castaway gods is an interesting question: and we hear that somewhere in the city is a large temple that is now given up to receiving all the gods from these converted temples. Besides schools there are other institutions raised for educational purposes.

The principal of these are perhaps the industrial and educational exhibits. This is an Exhibit of various manu-factured articles, which are supposed to be for sale. The admission is one copper, with an additional copper for entrance to the beauties of the Japanese room upstairs. Friday is reserved as ladies' day. The restriction in favour of ladies on this day is strictly observed, on account of Chinese usage. Husbands or male escorts have to wait outside.

While Tientsin is not noted for its temples, it has a few very interesting ones: perhaps the most beautiful is the memorial temple, dedicated to Li-Hung-Chang – the late Viceroy. This covers several acres of ground and has a beautiful pond with artistic bridges and little pavilions, making it one of the prettiest spots in Tientsin.

The entrance to the exhibition in the 'Industrial Meeting Grounds', as the Chinese characters have it

There has been great improvements made in Tientsin during the last ten years. It can be seen that the Chinese have not been slow to take full advantage of modern improvements introduced by foreign-ers. Yet there is one very important question not yet discussed to my satisfaction, and that is: precautions against fire. Outbreaks of fire are a usual occurrence in Tientsin and terrible damage is caused through this source. Bales of cotton – the most inflammable substance that it is

The memorial temple to Viceroy Li-Hung-Chang

A bridge and pavilion at
the memorial temple

possible to conceive – are stored up in large open compounds, some-times quite close to a factory where a spark is likely at any moment to set the lot in flames. During my stay in Tientsin there were no less than six outbreaks of fire, chiefly from this source. This is in the foreign Concessions alone. As regards the native city, not a month passes without a fire breaking out somewhere.

One very exciting fire which broke out occurred during a dust storm. Cotton compounds in the concession caught fire and the flames from it, in addition to flying pieces of burning cotton, set several other compounds alight. All the fire engines both in the concessions and the native city turned out but were of little or no use in bringing so many fires under control. Many houses were burnt to the ground. All the military were turned out to render assistance in removing cotton and property. The last compound which caught fire was quite close to a large kerosine oil store. This caused terrible excitement. Everyone expected the oil store to catch fire at any moment, which if it had, and with such a storm raging, the foreign Concessions might have been gutted. However the oil store luckily did not catch fire, and with the assistance of all the fire engines, troops and civilians, the fire was got under control about 5 p.m. in the afternoon, the outbreak occurring in the early morning.

Reflections on the Viceroy in the Lotus Pond

A cotton store ablaze: afterwards rebuilt as a barracks for the American troops

A large go-down or store containing an enormous amount of this inflammable substance was the scene of another exciting outbreak. This store, being in close proximity to the British magazine, which contained hundreds of pounds of high explosives, caused terrible excitement in the Concessions. The authorities, realising the extreme danger, turned out all the foreign troops to get the magazine emptied without delay.

Fighting the fire

It was very striking here to see so many different nationalities at work. They did not know what one and another were talking about: yet, they all realised the danger and the necessity of having the magazine emptied at all costs, without delay. With such a combined community the magazine was soon cleared, which ended excitement from this direction. The fire engines did fairly good work, but were not able to cope with such a conflagration. Fortunately, no other buildings caught fire, and, with the exception of the store which was burned to the ground, very slight damage was done. This large store was afterwards rebuilt and converted into a barracks for the United States Infantry, which arrived in Tientsin owing to the troubles.

The rickshaw is a very common vehicle all over China and has been in use for ages. The present day rickshaw – with its pneumatic tyred wheels – is a marked improvement on the old high-wheeled, steel rimmed bone-shaker, better known as 'Jingling Johnny' from the noise it creates when travelling over the paved streets. This vehicle has perhaps become more popular in Tientsin than in any other part of China. From the number that run the streets here, one could easily imagine that about half the coolie class earn their living in this way. The rubber-tyred vehicle was introduced by the foreigners, many of whom make quite a little business out of it. They keep a large stock, which they hire out to the coolies at about 60 cents to a dollar (say, one shilling and eightpence) per day. Those rickshaws are used mostly by the foreign population, the old type being used by the natives in the native quarter.

James Hutchinson in a rickshaw, with an obliging coolie

The rubber-tyred rickshaw is a very comfortable vehicle to sit in and, with a good coolie in the shafts, one can travel very fast. There was always a plentiful supply of coolies outside the Barracks gate, as both officers and other ranks were their best customers. The coolies who take up this business are very tormenting in the way that they push business, especially to one who is out for a constitutional walk. They seem to think that the foreigner is a very lazy sort of individual who requires their carriage at all times. The rickshaw trade has such an opposition in Tientsin that the coolies find it hard to make a living out of it after paying hiring expenses etc. Consequently they will follow one for hours in the hopes of being employed. By letting the first one know that you do not require him only means having another at your heels, till at last, rather than be continually pested with them, you employ one. They are very clever individuals and carry an ample supply of counterfeit money which they pass on to one in change if he is not careful, especially at night.

Some Tientsinese

The native population of Tientsin has been variously estimated at from 600,000 to over a million. It is very thickly populated. In 1904 the police attempted a census: but this was in terms of *chia* – families – and was not satisfactory. The best authorities (who can only guess) put the figure, including foreign settlements and the immediate suburbs, at about a million. Of these possibly only one half are of Tientsinese descent, and about one third of the whole come from other places in this province.

4 *Peking*

DURING my stay in North China I of course paid a visit to the capital of the oldest Empire on Earth, namely Peking, and will endeavour to help you to learn as much as possible about this historic city. Three thousand years ago, this wonderful town was not in the same position as now, and as China changes under the new spirit which is working within her, Peking shows more and more the effect of the various influences which have been brought to bear upon it. The retention of ancient buildings and customs forming a background to the modern institutions, which at the present time include well managed railways, telegraphs, post offices and street letter boxes, completes a picture which even picturesque Stamboul[24] cannot boast. As I have just said, for three thousand years the great city has been the heart[25] of a great nation; but since the Boxer Rising of 1900, the changes which have taken place are no doubt somewhat marvellous. In the first place railways have opened to the world the Imperial home of a great and ancient dynasty; macadamised roads run through its length and breadth, telegraph wires are brushed by leaves of trees growing where no foreigner was supposed to tread.

Before the railway to Peking was opened, travellers wishing to reach the capital had to travel either by boat on the Grand Canal, or across country in a country cart. It is only about 65 miles to Peking [from Tientsin]. To accomplish this distance by water took about five days. An ample supply of food had to be taken for the journey. The boat used had a sort of house built on it. The fore part of this house was for the passengers, the after part for the crew. They are merely sam-pans. Sails were used when the wind was favourable, but when it was ahead the men had to get out and drag it along the bank. This mode of travelling suited the Chinese alright, but to the foreigner it proved very wearisome and uncomfortable. During the winter months when the canal got frozen, the boats were converted into sledges by having two long spars attached to their bottoms: they are driven over the ice by a coolie who stands behind with a spear which he sticks in the ice. Travelling to Peking during this period required an ample supply of

---

[24] Istanbul

[25] But not of course as capital city throughout that time: the Ming dynasty moved their capital from Nanking to Peking in 1421. Bosworth notes that the name Peking (which means northern capital) was only in use from the early Ming dynasty onwards. Previously, the city was of some importance but mainly from AD 1000 or so, first serving as a major city or capital for non-Chinese 'invasion' dynasties such as the Mongols.

clothes and rugs; even then one would be almost frozen before ever reaching the capital.

The country cart was even more uncomfortable. No doubt it was quicker, but the jolting over the bad roads and tracks, in addition to the quantity of dust which arises, made one's journey such as would not easily have been forgotten.

The Chinese cart is the common means of road travel and is in use all over the Empire. It is a very clumsy vehicle. Its two wheels are twice as heavy as those of the carts used in our country. The shafts are about half as thick as telegraph poles and the bed of the carts rests upon them without any springs. Above the bed is a framework covered with blue canvas, which forms the roof of the cart. This is too low to allow for a seat, so one has to sit down in the bottom of the cart; there being no support for the back, it feels very uncomfortable; and to lie down, the bed is so short that one's feet would hang out at the front, disturbing the driver. Usually each cart is pulled by two shabby mules, one harnessed behind the other and driven by a Chinaman, who sits on the shafts. The mules go on a trot and one's flesh is almost jolted to jelly by the ruts in the road. The Chinese roads are merely tracks: they have been so much cut up by the travelling of carts during the ages that one would imagine he was going over hedges; the dust being so thick during dry weather adds greatly to the discomfort of the journey.

The Chinese country cart of the day

Ponies are about the most comfortable means of travelling when one is lucky enough to secure one. One can travel in China very cheap in a wheelbarrow. This seems a curious vehicle to travel on, but they have been used in China for ages for this purpose though, lately, they are much out of date. A wheelbarrow carries two passengers, one on either side. Two coolies are required, one in the shafts while the other drags it.

Since the railway was opened, travelling to Peking is only a matter of a few hours. Even the Chinese have abandoned the old method and taken full advantage of the foreigner's invention. The Chinese officials were at first afraid to allow the construction of a railroad for fear of the anger of the boat owners and cart drivers: those individuals do not agree with the inventions of foreigners to do away with their facilities of earning a living. The railway from Peking to Tientsin is a section of the Imperial Railway: its terminus is at Peking and it runs through to Moukden where it connects up with the Trans-Siberian route to Europe.

Peking lies 39 degrees 55 minutes northern latitude and 116 degrees 25 minutes longitude east of Greenwich, or in the same latitude practically as Rome. Peking has been open in effect to the foreigner since 1860 but it is only since 1900 that apart from diplomats, the foreign officials of the Imperial Maritime Customs, missionaries and a few privileged people, a large influx of Europeans took place. There is also now a strong contingent of Japanese.

The population of Peking, composed of Chinese, Mongolians and Manchus, is estimated as being between 600,000 and 1,000,000. The Chinese Government recently had a census taken of the families in the city and this shows that the Inner or Tartar City contains 79,000 families, while the outer or Chinese City contains 47,000 families: altogether 126,000 families. Mr Rockhill, the late American Minister to China, calculated according to the published reports of the Royal Geographical Association that each family contained 5.5 heads which (in round figures) means that Peking has a population of 700,000 inhabitants.

The City Walls

The first glimpse we get of Peking when travelling by rail from Tientsin[26] is the blackened walls of the Chinese City, showing up prominently against its background, the pale blue sky. One first passes through these outer walls, along by the south wall of the Tartar City and then we find ourselves at a standstill at the Ch'ien-Men terminus – outside the Tartar City wall on the east side of its central main gate, but inside the walls of the Chinese City. Here one finds himself in the centre of 'small-eyed China's crockery ware metropolis'. After leaving the train one is confronted by two different ways to enter the city, either the Ch'ien-Men Gate or the Small Water Gate, Hsiao-Shui-Men, which brings one into the centre of the Legation Quarter.

The city of Peking is rectangular in shape, running from north to south. Here we can see cities within cities, each city being surrounded by its own wall. It is divided into two sections: the northern section, known as the Tartar or main city[27], contains the Tartar or Manchu population: that is the same race as the dynasty. The southern section – known as the Chinese or Outer city – contains the Chinese population.

The outer walls which engirdle the city of Peking have a total length of 24½ miles. They are composed of two portions, namely the present walls of the more ancient Tartar or Manchu city which were built in AD 1421[28], and those of the Chinese city which were built 123 years later[29]. Within the Tartar City is the walled Imperial City. And in the heart of this, within another wall, stands the proud and powerful Forbidden City of China. The Tartar City wall has a total length of over 41 Chinese *li* or fourteen English miles. It is a structure 41 feet in

[26]   This was the case in Hutchinson's time, but no longer: most of the walls described have since been almost completely dismantled. Some of the gates remain or have been rebuilt.

[27]   Known as such perhaps from 1644 onward, that being the date when the Manchus seized power from the Chinese (Ming) dynasty.

[28]   In fact the Ming dynasty basically completed their construction of these Inner (later, Tartar) City walls about 1439.

[29]   This would be more accurately stated at about 1553.

The wall of the Chinese City, Peking, with the railway running alongside

height, at its base the width is sixty-two feet, and at the top it measures about fifty feet. There are nine gates to the Tartar city: two in the north wall, two in the east, two in the west, and three in the south wall.

The Chinese City has to the east, west and south its own walls, while to the north it is cut off from the Tartar City by the latter's southern wall. The Chinese City walls were built in AD 1544. The Chinese City is the commercial part of Peking. The great Ch'ien-Men Street which runs from the Ch'ien-Men Gate to the Temple of Heaven is the principal street. Here the largest Chinese book and picture stores are situated, also large silk, fur and curio shops. The Chinese city wall is 9½ miles in length (exclusive of the Tartar City South wall). It is a structure only 25 feet in height, with a base of about 20 feet in thickness. This city has in all ten gates (including the three gates of the Tartar City).

The plan of Peking reminds me of the New Jerusalem and yet one cannot see how any connection between them could arise. 'The city lieth four-square, and the length is as large as the breadth' and 'had a wall great and high'. In both cases the walls face each to a point in the compass. In the number of gates the resemblance ceases, for Peking has as one of its titles 'City of the Nine Gates'.

Looking back to the early history of China, to the days of Kublai-Khan or the thirteenth century when this city of Peking was built, gives one an insight of how such strongholds came to be built around the Imperial palace. The Tartar conquerors who at that time designed this palace[30] had with good purpose made their Imperial residence a last citadel in the huge city of Peking, a citadel which could be easily

---

[30] Michael Bosworth notes that, while the Mongols indeed built a palace on or near the site of the Forbidden City, the palace which Hutchinson goes on to describe was built by the Chinese Ming dynasty rulers in the early 15th century, on top of the Mongol ruins.

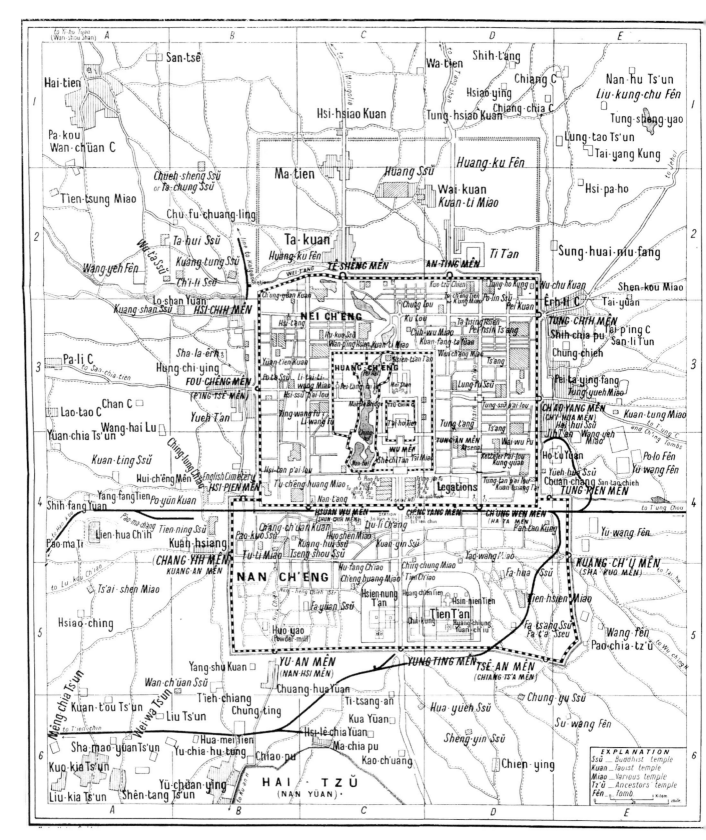

Peking and the immediately surrounding area

From Madrolle's Guide Books: Northern China, The Valley of the Blue River, Korea; Hachette & Company, 1912; by courtesy of the Perry-Castañeda Library
Map Collection, University of Texas

defended to the death in the old days, even when the enemy had seized all the outer walls. For without powerful cannon, the place was impregnable.

In 1860 a foreign residence was forced upon the Chinese Government at the point of the bayonet, and places to live in were required. The locality selected was the south-east section of the Tartar City. The foreign legations since 1900 have exclusive quarters of their own.

The Foreign Legations

Up till 1900 the Legation quarters had the appearance of a mixed Chinese and foreign settlement. Here were the residences of the foreign Ministers and those of the princes, mandarins and influential natives. There was also the famous library of the Hanlin Academy, the oldest university in the world, within the legation grounds. Since the Boxer troubles of 1900, the Legation quarter has been exclusive to foreign diplomats, the foreign banks, agencies and a few privileged foreigners. In its present aspect the Legation Quarter has the appearance of a fortress of rectangular shape. Its southern end is enclosed by the great Tartar city wall between the Hata-men Gate on the eastern extremity and the Ch'ien-men on the western, while its northern end is enclosed by the fortress-like wall along the so-called Legation Glacis. This rectangular section is divided up by few streets, the principal one of which is Legation Street, which runs east to west through the whole length of Legation Quarter. Through the centre section from south to north runs Canal Street: here the Imperial Canal of Peking crosses Legation Quarter. The canal is called *Canal du Jade*, but its name 'Yue-Ho' means Imperial Canal. Canal Street has at its southern end a sign describing it as *Quai du Congrès*. The canal, which is the central part of the Legation Quarter, has now its own gate, the so-called Hsiao-Shui-Men, which means the Small Water Gate, by which visitors can enter the Legation Quarter after leaving their train, the terminus of the Imperial Railway being situated just outside.

Referring back to the troubles of 1900, before this gate was opened, when the Legation quarters were besieged by the Boxers, the international troops – after the fall of Tientsin – marched on Peking to relieve the Legations, fighting the whole way up. On arrival at Peking they found it impossible to make an entrance by any of the gates, as the Chinese had lined the walls, from which they opened a deadly fire. The British column which marched on the southern section of the Chinese City got in unmolested by scaling the wall and, forcing their way through the Chinese City, entered through the sluice gate underneath where the Small Water Gate now stands, and relieved the Legations. The Boxers, when they saw the foreign troops in the Legation, fled.

The Officers of the Legation Guards and Attachés, Peking 1910
From the album of Col. W. H. Crawford, Regimental Museum of the Royal Inniskilling Fusiliers, Enniskillen

1st Row (in front). Capt. Leah; Capt. Collardet; Sub.-Capt. von Sharenberg; Lt. de la Rochebrochard; Lt. Vecchiato; Lt. Grazioli; 2/Lt. Takata; Lt. Pudsey; Lt. Kawamura; Capt. Holden; Sub.-Lt. Ciani

2nd Row. Lt. Hirata; Lt. Kuhlmann; Lt. Coraggio; Capt. Smythe; Lt.-Col. Barnett; Col. Korniloff; Major-Genl. Aoki; Col. Abbot Anderson; Lt. Col. Willoughby; Capt. Mallinarich; Capt. Spagna; Capt. Dinkelmann; Major Pernot; Lt. Yagi

3rd Row. Lt. Lambert; Lt. Leblanc; Lt. Manzoni; Capt. Steward; Lt. Vianelli; Major Jones; Capt. di Giura; Capt. Thornhill; Capt. Drevet; Capt. Clarke; Major Honjo; Lt. Paarmann; Lt. Cream; Lt. Ockermuller; Capt. Savin

4th Row. Capt. FitzHugh; Capt. Brooke; Lt. Waller; Capt. Holcombe; Lt. McConnell; Dr. Owens; Capt. Nozaki; Lt. Paoli; Capt. Kremenetzky; Capt. Matziersky; Dr. Schmidt; Paymaster Hartlieb; Lt. Crespi

Like the Concessions in Tientsin, the Legations in Peking are miniatures with modifications of the countries that they represent. The British Legation being an exception so far as the Minister's residence is concerned, this being about the first Legation quarter to be established in Peking. It is only since 1900 that the other Legations have been

completed to their present state. The following are the names of the foreign Legations in Peking: British, French, German, American, Italian, Russian, Japanese, Spanish, Austro-Hungarian, Portuguese, Belgian, and Denmark. Brazil, Cuba and Sweden will soon have their Legation quarters also. From this long list it will be seen that one meets in Peking a representative of nearly every nationality in the world.

Top:
Canal Street and the Water Gate, Peking: (on the left, the southern end of the Wagon-Lits Hotel)

Above:
The sluice-gate where British troops forced an entry to the Legation Quarter to rescue trapped foreign residents and Chinese Christians

The first Legation we arrive at after passing through Ch'ien-Men is that of the Americans. This Legation is a plain but imposing building and by what we could see, they had probably the most comfortable quarters of any Legation. In the main building resides the Minister, and residential buildings have been erected for the First and Second Secretaries and the Interpreter. The Military Attaché and the students attached to the Legation live in a temple just west of the Small Water Gate.

Next we come to the Austro-Hungarian Legation which has the most commodious residence and is situated on the highest point in Legation Quarter. There are two pavilions for the residences of the Secretaries and the Legation staff. The inner garden terrace and the main entrance to this Legation on Maria Theresa Street, which stand in front of the Minister's residence, are very attractive. Along the western wall of the garden is a small chapel where Commander Thomann, late Frigate-Captain in the Austro-Hungarian Navy, and a number of bluejackets who fell in 1900 are buried.

We now pass into the Belgian Legation and we see a fine artistic fence of iron which separates the Legation from Legation Street. The main building is a copy of one of King Leopold's villas in Brussels. There are four pavilions which serve as residences for the Secretaries etc.

A bird's eye view of the British Legation

Now we come to our own Legation, the British Legation. It was originally the palace of one of the princes of the dynasty, and was leased to the British Government as a residence for our British Minister. There is a high wall surrounding the ground, which encloses about three acres: and, according to the theory of European International Law, it is British soil. The palace may be described as a miniature of the Great Imperial Palace, the halls being fewer in number and smaller in size: they are all arranged on a line running north and south. There are other residences for the accommodation of the Secretaries, interpreters and officials connected with the Legation. At the north-west corner are some buildings known as 'the Students' Quarters'. Young gentlemen coming out for the Chinese Consular Service have first to learn the language. This they do in Peking, and it requires two or three years study under native teachers. The Legation Guard barracks is situated close to the Students' Quarters: here the British military detachment reside.

Just in front of the main gate stands a small marble obelisk with the simple inscription '20th June to 14th August 1900'; and also further down we see some printing which is almost obliterated. The words are 'Lest we forget' and remind one of the events of 1900 when the Legation Quarter was besieged by the Boxers. On entering the compound one stands in an avenue of tall and stately trees, to the right of which are two big entrance gates (one after another in Chinese palace or temple form). They are of interesting celestial architecture. In the rear of them stands the Minister's residence, a Chinese *yamen*. There are also a number of residential and office buildings and a chapel. Passing straight down the avenue we come to the quarters of the British Detachment of troops, whose quarters are known as the British Legation Guard. We walked around the Glacis and found that all the loopholes were blocked up, but, if trouble started, we were informed that the soldiers would soon knock away the obstruction. These loopholes were opened during the late Revolution, but fortunately did not have to be used.

We next pass into the Russian Legation which is in close contact to the British. The Russians have a strongly built residence: it is a pretty building and very commodious. In the grounds we also see offices and buildings for the Secretaries and staff. Each official has his own residence and there is a chapel attached to the Legation.

We now move along Legation Street and enter the French Legation, where we observe a number of pretty buildings erected in French architecture. The Minister's residence is a palatial structure and the Secretaries, Military Attaché and the two Interpreters each have their own residence; and in the grounds we also see a small chapel surrounded by a pretty lawn and garden.

Leaving and crossing to the other side of Legation Street we come to the German Legation and here we find the prettiest garden of all the Legations. The buildings are partly new and partly reconstructed, the

A sentry guards the British Minister's Residence

Foreign diplomats and Ch'ing Dynasty officials[31]

new portions being of German architecture. On this ground stands the old Peking Club which is now used by the Legation.

Taking one of the bye-streets we come out into Canal Street where we arrive at the Japanese Legation, which, like the Japanese Concession in Tientsin, is making rapid advancement towards improvement. This Legation has a new semi-foreign Japanese Palace for the use of its Minister and a Japanese gardener has perfected a very attractive Japanese garden. The main building has on its lower floor a large and ornamented reception room as well as many other quarters for entertainment. Among these is a dining room where from 100 to 150 persons can be seated, and here also is the Minister's study, a billiard room and a card room. The whole of the lower floor walls are excellently decorated. The large hall leading to the marble staircase can be used for dancing when entertainment takes place. On the upper floor are the Minister's private rooms and a section of this floor is decorated in *tatami* and, with its pretty straw mat floorings, it has a very attractive appearance.

Now we pass on to the Italian Legation. Here we find the main building is built in Italian style and a miniature of the Palazzo Farnese of Rome. In the spacious grounds stand pavilions, office buildings, a church and conservatory. Also we observe a Marconi wireless telegraph station which can communicate with the Italian men-of-war when cruising in the Gulf of Pei-Chih-Li.

The other Legations are those of the Mexicans, Netherlands, Portuguese and the Spanish. These are all small Legations and have not any buildings of importance. I might just say that the Spanish Legation occupies the same building as it did before 1900 and did not suffer from the Boxers. It is a Chinese-European *yamen*.

The Wagons-Lits, the largest hotel in Peking, is situated in Canal Street. Opposite the British Legation, this building was only completed in 1910. All tourists on a visit to Peking take quarters in this hotel.

Further along Canal Street, close to the British Legation wall, stands the blockhouse where a gallant attempt was made by a British

---

[31] Bosworth believes that the Chinese official seated lower left in this photograph, which Hutchinson may not have taken personally, is Tuan Ch'i-jui (Duan Qirui in today's parlance). Duan would have been in Peking in 1910 and most of 1911: he had been left there, as one of his top lieutenants in the Beiyang (Northern) Army clique, by Yuan Shikai who was on enforced 'sick-leave'. Duan had been one of the first cadets to enrol in the Beiyang Military Academy in 1881. He went on to study in Germany and to be appointed head of the New Army's artillery by Yuan Shikai. He was loyal to Yuan during the revolution of 1911 as a commander and then a military governor. When Yuan died in 1916 Duan became Premier. Bosworth also surmises that the German officer seated on the right was Alfred Meyer-Waldeck, who assumed his duties as the (last) German Governor of Kiautschou on August 19, 1911. The Governors there were all naval personnel.

officer and three men with a Maxim gun to keep the furious Boxers at bay. A terrible mishap occurred here during this attempt, which proved fatal to the three soldiers, the officer only escaping. An iron door which leads from the blockhouse into the Legation was left in charge of a sentry. This sentry through excitement or some unknown reason locked the door and quit his post, not thinking of the four men who were manning the blockhouse outside. The officer and three men, when their ammunition ran short, made an effort to retire into the Legation, and the door being locked they were murdered outside. The officer, who was fortunate in scaling the wall, escaped. A portion of the wall still remains shattered and bears the inscription 'Lest we forget' as a memento.

By taking a walk along the top of the city wall between the Ch'ien-men and Hata-men Gates, one gets a splendid view of all the Legation compounds. This promenade is greatly used by the foreigners and is furnished with garden seats where one can take a rest in comfort high above Peking's busy thoroughfares. The Germans and Americans whose Legation quarters are close beneath the wall have built magazines for the storage of ammunition on the top of the wall, with an underground passage connecting them with their respective Legations. Here a large stock of ammunition is stored and guarded by a sentry. This is an emergency supply in case at any time the walls should have to be manned. Since the siege of 1900 every precaution has been taken to ensure that such a disastrous event will not occur again.

As there are no amusements or attractions in Peking for Europeans, they have to find them among themselves. Most of the Legations

The Wagon-Lits Hotel as it was when completed in 1910

The blockhouse near
the British Legation

contain reading rooms, billiard rooms etc and a skating pool for the winter. The British troops stationed there have their own reading and billiard rooms. Trips to the various temples and places of interest are arranged weekly, when a sort of picnic takes place. It is advisable to take some form of conveyance or else hire a pony. The different troops generally hire donkeys and it is amusing to see them riding on donkeys, travelling about in large squads through the streets of Peking on these occasions: the price they are charged is about 40 cents or eightpence for the whole afternoon. Donkeys are about the best means of reaching the various temples outside the city, as very often 'cross country' has to be taken. Rickshaws are sometimes employed but in most cases the roads are too bad for rickshaws and to reach these places in any vehicle means walking half the way. They cost about 15 cents (threepence) per hour or a dollar for the whole day.

If we walk to the Y.M.C.A. in Hata-Men Street we shall find a lot of boys there with donkeys for hire. Each of us having seized a donkey, we make a bargain and agree to pay each boy 10 cents an hour for his 'mount', which is not much larger than a Newfoundland dog: they are much smaller animals than those of this country. The saddles are merely a number of blankets piled on their backs and so strapped that they stand out like flat boards. The stirrups are heavy iron rings tied to the blankets with pieces of rope. The bridles are as curious in their aspect. The Chinese seldom use bridles on donkeys and the average Chinese donkey does not understand the use of the bit. He is accustomed to being directed this way or that by a blow on the neck with a club. When a foreigner hires a donkey he gets a bridle on and by giving the boy a few extra cents he will run after him the whole way and act as driver: we have no driving to do.

A squadron of soldiers belonging to the various Legations, with their mixture of uniforms, travelling through the streets with as many boys running behind whistling and shouting at the steeds, make a sight very striking and humorous. I was a member of one of those squadrons on various occasions and had some exciting times. The traffic on the streets of Peking is not regulated. Consequently carts, rickshaws and pedestrians seem to go where they like and stop where they like – the result being a hopeless state of confusion in which we got entangled. Numerous times we got mixed up with all sorts of vehicles. Our steeds being very stubborn and not used to the bit made matters even worse.

On one occasion my steed took me at full speed through a shop door, knocking down the proprietor's display of goods which were neatly arranged on both sides of the entrance. Fortunately very little harm was done and should I have understood the shop-keeper's language, I could relate the welcome I received for entering his premises with such a comrade. Such are the foreigner's experiences in Peking and which help to occupy a good deal of the soldier's spare time. Football and other matches with each other and with members of the other Legations are got up; dinners and other social entertainments are also frequent and thus life is made tolerable to those whose fate it is to live in this far-away land. Fortunately the best feelings exist between the members of the various Legations, and the intercourse resulting from it helps to make a dull life pleasant. During my stay in Peking I accomplished my tour inside the walls in the rickshaw. My visits to the outer suburbs and their places of interest was made on my former friend – the donkey.

I have already given an account of the walls of this most wonderful 'Celestial' City. Inside and outside these walls are many places of interest including temples of Buddha, Confucius[32], Mencius[33] and Lamas. In addition to Mahomedan mosques and pagodas of every description[34], all of which China is the slave.

The Tartar City

This part of Peking is called 'Nei-Ch'eng' or inner city. As stated above, the rectangular extent of the wall of this city covers over

A kerbside market stall

---

[32]　K'ung-fu-tzu in the Wade-Giles orthography, 551–479 BC, thinker whose philosophy emphasized personal and governmental morality, correctness of social relationships, justice and sincerity.

[33]　4th century BC Confucian philosopher.

[34]　The lamas being priests of one sect of Buddhism, and the pagodas parts of Buddhist temple complexes.

41 Chinese *li* or fourteen English miles and its walls were built in AD 1421.

Before dealing with places of interest in the Tartar City, it would not be out of place to give a short description of the Ch'ien-men or Main Gate to this city of Manchu celestials. The Ch'ien-men Gate is situated in the centre of the south wall of the Tartar City. It is the main thoroughfare between the two cities. This gate, being close to the Legation quarter, was destroyed during the troubles of 1900 but was rebuilt again at a cost of one million *teals*[35]. The new Ch'ien-men lies in front of the main entrance to the Imperial and Forbidden cities. It has, like the other eight large gates of the Tartar City, its fortress-shaped entrances and divisions. Through the Ch'ien-men an enormous amount of traffic takes place comprising horses, mules, donkeys, camels, carriages, carts, sedan chairs, rickshaws, human carriers etc, in addition to the great state processions of the Emperor, when going to worship in the Temple of Heaven. The gates of Peking are closed during the night, except the Ch'ien-Men and 'Water Gate'.

The Ch'ien-men Gate rebuilt

The two main streets of the Tartar City, namely the Shun-Chi-men and Hata-men Streets, run north and south, parallel with the city walls. All gates and halls are also on the axis of a line running north and south. This is the case with all palaces, *yamens* or official residences, houses and temples in China. The buildings attached to the great tomb of Yung-Lê – the most important of the Ming tombs – are also arranged on the same plan, showing a continuity of idea carried

[35] The silver *teal* was a Chinese high-value currency.

A tall ship off the rocky island of Malta

Street-scene in the German Concession in Tientsin

A German gun-boat moored on the Pei-Ho River

James Hutchinson and fellow NCO on a gun captured during the Boxer Rebellion

The Broken Column, commemorating the Japanese soldiers who fell in 1900

Victoria Park and its bandstand, where the expatriates of Tientsin would meet

A main street in Tientsin's Native City

Advertising, Tientsin-style

A storeyed bridge at the Imperial Summer Palace

The famed marble Boat House at the Imperial Summer Palace

Peking's Temple of Heaven

Caged birds remain a pastime among older men in today's Beijing

A wheelbarrow load for market

The Peking to Kalgan train enters a tunnel

A panoramic view at the Imperial Summer Palace

Another marvel with marble

The beautiful Myriad Buddhas Temple

Another view of the Temple of the Myriad Buddhas, also known as the Temple of Buddhist Virtue (*Fo-Hsiang-Ko*)

though each. The popular way of understanding this arrangement is that it is a reference to the *'feng-shui'* [36], a very peculiar deification of wind and water, which occupies a large place in the common superstitions of this country. The cold wind (and in Peking in winter it is a biting, frosty wind) comes from the north. The solid wall, with no door or entrance on that side, is a safeguard against this. From the south, on the contrary, the warmth of the sun is felt: and hence the house, the house of the dead, and the temple are all made so as to face this genial part of the heavens. The Christian church is built with reference to the rising sun; and the Temple of Solomon was the same, although, strangely enough, instead of placing the altar on the east, the entrance opened out so that the sun's rays would shine in as it rose. The plan of the Chinese temples suggests that they had a reference to the sun in his meridian glory, his highest point of power and influence.

Hata-men Street contains many places of interest such as the Lama Temple, Temple of Confucius and Hall of Classics. Of these we will consider each in turn. Making an excursion in this direction one first passes the Ketteler Memorial. Referring back again to 1900, we are told that on this spot Baron von Ketteler – the German Minister to the Court of China – was shot from behind on June 20th, 1900. Resulting from his murder very serious correspondence passed between the German and Chinese Governments[37]. The Chinese Emperor, fearing a very serious result to follow, apologised to the German Emperor and had this structure of white marble erected. The memorial crosses the whole width of Hata-men Street. The inscription on the monument[38] is in German, Latin and Chinese. It states the history of the occurrence and the fact that the Emperor of China has erected this monument to the memory of Baron von Ketteler[39]. The translation of the inscription reads as follows: 'This monument, by command of the Emperor of China, has been erected in memory of the Imperial German Minister, Chevalier von Ketteler, who on this spot, by the villainous hand of a murderer, was killed on 20th June, 1900: for everlasting memory of his name; for continued proof of the anger of the Emperor for this atrocity; as a warning to all'.

The Lama Temple has many historic attractions and curiosities within its wall. In 1723 the palace which previously had stood on this

---

[36] Which one commentator describes as 'the Chinese art of placement', the essence of which is the creation of a harmony and dynamic balance between one's inner and exterior space.

[37] i.e. following the quelling of the Boxer Rebellion.

[38] Bosworth notes that the monument was dismantled following China's declaration of war on Germany in 1917. It was later reassembled minus the inscriptions and stands today in Zhongshan Park near the Forbidden City. It is now known as The Arch of the Triumph of Righteousness. Only the wooden, tiled top portion has been altered.

[39] Klemens August Freiherr von Ketteler 1853–1900 was German Plenipotentiary in Peking. He reacted strongly to the Boxers' violence and was killed in a firefight with Imperial Guards on June 20, 1900 when on his way to the Ministry of Foreign Affairs.

The monument erected by the Emperor to the memory of Baron von Ketteler

spot was turned into a temple by Emperor Yung-Cheng. The entrance into the temple is on the north section of Hata-Men Street. No sooner has a visitor passed the entrance than the gate-keeper asks for money, and a ten cent piece will generally satisfy him. A number of boys, some of whom speak two or three words of English, offer their services as guides and of course want money in return. When visiting places in China it is well for a visitor to have a good supply of 10 cent pieces, which act like magic and open a good many doors which otherwise would remain locked. When one finally enters the inner temple courts, the Lama priests very amiably ask for money and also want a 10 cent piece here and there. It is easy to see that they are fond of money and think Mr. Foreigner has 'plenty muchie money'.

This temple, like many others, is at present in a rather dilapidated condition. The temple compound is divided into several sections. In the main building is a colossal statue, 70 feet high, of the image of Maitreya Buddha, the incarnation of Buddha yet to come. Another 10 cent piece will enable one to gain permission to ascend the gallery running round the building, from which one can judge better the huge proportions of this image, which is supposed to be made from one piece of wood and was brought from Tibet. Everything about it is purely Indian, and the same may be said of the innumerable smaller figures of divinities which may be seen at this place, personating the Lohan or disciples of Buddha. A visitor can generally purchase one of the small brass lamps which stand before the big Buddha, if he is in search of souvenirs.

In the early morning and towards evening one can follow with interest the rites and ceremonies of hundreds of these priests. They all wear yellow vestments, yellow being the distinguishing colour of the dress of one sect of Buddhists. There are several classes of Lama priests: some of them come from Mongolia, others from Tibet and the northern parts of the Himalayas, and others from all parts of China. The high priest of this temple is a Tibetan and is called the Living

Buddha. The priests in this temple wear a very strange shaped yellow hat, which one could almost believe was copied from a Greek helmet. I visited this temple in the evening when they were performing an elaborate service. About thirty or forty were sitting in their yellow costume, chanting to the accompaniment of drums, cymbals, horns, gongs and bells. I could see a very small boy among the performers making faces at me, as small boys are wont to do everywhere. I tried to get a photograph of this yellow congregation but found it impossible owing to the darkness of such places for the want of windows.

In the court yard close by these main buildings are the large praying wheels with the prayers inscribed in Tibetan. A number of figures made from mud, more quaint than beautiful, are generally offered for sale to visitors. The large bronze and marble lions at the entrance court to the temple are also an object of admiration. Every visitor to the Lama Temple has an opportunity of looking at the numerous costly presents made to this temple by Emperors and Princes. They are of *cloisonné*, precious metals and other materials.

The Confucian Temple is situated a few hundred paces from the Lama Temple. This bears the general appearance of all Confucian temples in China. All around is very quiet and on entering the first compound we see hundreds of immense stone monuments inscribed with Chinese and Manchu lettering[40]. In the main building stands a tablet in memory of Confucius, the Chinese sage, also the tablets of Mencius and other Chinese philosophers. The temple also contains some quaint old stone drums, which they call Hsi-Ku and which are said to be 2,000 years old and were made during the Chou Dynasty 1122–256 B C.

On each side of the gateway, under small kiosks with roofs of blue tiles, stand big carved stone monuments. These monuments are placed on top of huge stone tortoises. I might mention here that the tortoise is one of the sacred animals of the Chinese. The monuments are inscribed with an account of the successful wars which took place under the Emperors K'ang-Hsi, Yung-Cheng and Ch'ien-Lung.

Just north of the Imperial City stand two very high towers, known by distinction as the Bell and Drum Towers. From the top platform of the Bell Tower there is a pretty view towards the north-eastern hills and the country lying outside of the northern wall. The tower contains one of the five great bells

One of the 'kiosks' at
the Confucian Temple gateway

[40]   The complex described by Hutchinson actually includes both the Confucian Temple and the Imperial College. Most of the lettering on the stone monuments in the courtyard contains the names of candidates successful in the Imperial Civil Service exams in given years.

Peking's Bell Tower

which were cast under Emperor Yung-Lê about AD 1411 during the Ming Dynasty. There are many tales told about the casting of this great bell. The bell founder's daughter, it is told, jumped into the glowing red hot metal when this enormous bell weighing 120,000 pounds was cast. It is believed that this action brought about the success of the casting, but the poor bell founder lost his mind through the loss of his daughter. The bell is struck by the watchman at 8 p.m. daily. So many tales are told about the ancient Chinese, it is hard to say what is really the truth. One thing certain is that the ancient Chinese possessed many secrets in the manufacture of bells and other things which are now almost lost. The fine tone which the ancient Chinese bells possess cannot be got now-a-days. The observation platform where the great bell is stands about 130 feet above the street level.

The Drum Tower is near the central part of the north wall of the Tartar City and we found it worthwhile tipping the keeper to allow us to go to the top of this tall tower. We had to climb seventy-five steps of rather uncomfortable proportion, but on arriving at the top we were rewarded with a most picturesque view of Peking and its surroundings. Directly south one observes the Coal Hill and many of the Palaces of the Forbidden City, while the Temple of Heaven, the Hata-Men, the Department of War and the western hills and other distant points make a splendid panorama of Peking and its suburbs. There are three large drums inside the great hall of the tower, which daily at 9 p.m. announce the hour of rest by being beaten with 108 strokes. Also at 1 a.m. the watchman strikes them. The height of the great drum hall is also 130 feet above street

The Drum Tower

level. What those towers were built for it is hard to say, but I take it that they were look-out towers, from their high position in the north of the city, the bell and drums being used to give warning of the approach of an enemy.

The Imperial City

We now reach the walled Imperial City – an inner section of the Tartar City. The wall of this city is about six miles in circumference, 18 feet high but only 6½ feet thick. This wall is quite different to those of the other cities: they are built of dirty coloured bricks, but the wall of the Imperial City is built with red bricks and the top is finished off with artistic yellow tiles. There are four gates facing north, south, east and west. Along the east side is the Tung-An-Men gate and on the west side the Hsi-An-Men, and to the south is the Ta-Ch'ing-Men. This gate attracts the sight of all who enter the Ch'ien-Men as it is situated just in front of this central south gate of the Tartar City. This gate is also passed when going from the southwest part of the Tartar City to the Legation Quarter. The north gate of the Imperial City stands in front of the Bell and Drum Towers, this gate is the Ti-An-Men and also the Hou-Men, which means the rear gate. Some parts of the Imperial City cannot be visited.

Other sections can be freely walked through: the Hsi-An-Men or west gate gives free access, from where one can get a good view of the palaces in the Forbidden City with their yellow tiled roofs: yellow being the Imperial colour and held in such high esteem with the Chinese that only buildings such as Imperial residences and temples founded by Imperial sanction are allowed to have yellow roofs. The Emperor himself is sometimes styled 'The Yellow Lord'. Processions of every description, weddings and funerals would not receive their sacred dignity unless yellow formed the chief colour. The idols and interior of all temples have the same yellow tint – which goes to show that the colour figures highly in the superstitions of the race.

The western section of the Imperial City cannot be visited, at least that section which forms the 'Winter Palace' or pleasure grounds of the 'Three Oceans'. Here three small lakes exist from which the palace derives its name. The Summer Palace is situated about eight miles in a north-westerly direction from Peking and a magnificent place it is: this, however, we will consider later. It will be seen that the Emperor and the Imperial court have special palaces in which to dwell during different seasons of the year.

The Forbidden City

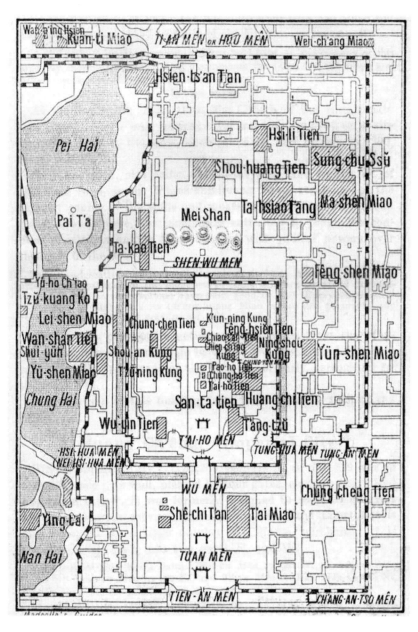

Map of Peking's Forbidden City
From Madrolle's Guide Books: Northern China, The
Valley of the Blue River, Korea; Hachette & Company,
1912; by courtesy of the
Perry-Castañeda Library Map Collection,
University of Texas

Close to the Winter Palace stands a bottle-shaped pagoda which is in the charge of Lama priests. It is 270 feet high and was built about seven centuries ago. A stairway leads up to a platform and it takes one to be careful how he ascends as they are partly in ruins. From this platform one can get a look into the Forbidden City and a good view of the Imperial City. The platform is partly in ruins and writings on the wall show that some French were located here during the troubles of 1900. The Pei-T'ang Cathedral with other adjoining religious institutions, situated close by inside the west gate, is the principal seat of the Catholic organisations of China. Under the great K'ang Hsi in AD 1693 the Roman Catholic mission was given the privilege of building a church in this section of Peking. However the late Empress Dowager wished the original seat of the Pei-T'ang removed, as the old church building overlooked the Imperial pleasure grounds of the San Hai or Three Oceans. The negotiations between Rome and Peking about the removal of the old Pei-T'ang were carried on for many years until in 1888 this new building was erected. The old one was then used as a museum until 1909, when it was demolished. During the troubles of 1900 the French and Italians made a heroic defence of this cathedral, in which the late Bishop Favier[41], with his clergy and thousands of Chinese Christians took refuge. The graves of many who fell in this defence in 1900 are in the French cemetery close by.

The last occasion on which foreigners (except the foreign Ministers) were known to enter the Forbidden City was in 1900, after the relief of the Legations when the Empress Dowager and her court fled. Foreign officers on that occasion entered the palaces and ransacked them. It was here that some documents were discovered which gave a clue to the effect that the Empress Dowager and her officials were the instigation of the Boxer troubles.

The foreign Ministers have to enter the Forbidden City on certain occasions to interview the Emperor. On such occasions they are escorted by their respective military guards to the entrance of the city, from where they are taken by Chinese authorities to the reception room. When in the Forbidden City the Minister must report to his guard every fifteen minutes that he is alright. The Emperor will not be responsible for the life of a Minister on these occasions.

The northern section of the Forbidden City is enclosed by a square wall, in the centre of which is an artificial hill about 210 feet high which is said to have been formed by a large amount of coal stored here under previous dynasties when war rumours were prevalent. This hill is commonly called 'Ching-Shan' or 'Mei-Shan', or 'Coal Hill'. Another version is that this so-called artificial hill was made from the earth and mud which was dug out of that part of the Forbidden City where the San Hai lakes in the Imperial pleasure ground now exist.

Being planted with trees and having pagodas and shrines erected on prominent points, it becomes a striking object in the City, attracting the eyes by its sudden elevation. According to history those kiosks, pagodas and shrines were built by Emperor Chia-Ching (1522–67). History further tells that in AD 1644, the last of the Ming Emperors, in despair, committed suicide here by

The 'White Dagoba' of the Miaoying Monastery

[41] Pierre Marie Alphonse Favier (1873–1905).

The Coal Hill enclosure

hanging himself in a tree. This was the result of a consultation he is supposed to have had with the gods of the San-Kwan-Miao Temple who told him to draw lots. If he should draw a large bamboo stick, he should attack the approaching foe, or if he should draw the middle bamboo stick, then he should await the enemy; but in the case of drawing the short bamboo he should commit suicide. On the northern foot of this hill stands the Kuan-Te-Tien, which spacious hall serves as mortuary after the death of a member of the Imperial family, until the remains are removed to the Imperial mausoleums at the Tung-Ling or the Hsi-Ling.

A broad moat and a high square brick wall make the division between the Imperial and Forbidden Cities. In the Forbidden City are the various Imperial palaces and buildings where the receptions of the Emperor are held, also the private residential quarters of the Court. The City has a length of 3,300 feet and a breadth of 2,579 feet. The wall is 22 feet high with four gates facing north, south, east and west. All around these walls on the outside of the city there is a military barracks. In the walls of this city there are only four gates and on each gate is posted a double sentry. Should any unauthorised person attempt to enter, the sentries will cross their rifles to prevent it.

The population of Peking proper is Tartar or Manchu: that is, it belongs to the same race as the Dynasty, and is not to be confused with the Chinese population which lives in a separate walled city on the south side. These Manchus are a military body, drilled, armed and organized accordingly. They constitute an army, a living bulwark, round the Emperor in his palace. They are equivalent to what in Europe would be called the Guard. It was to feed these unproductive soldiers that the 'Grand Canal' or 'Grain Tribute River' was made. They are paid and fed out of the Imperial resources, and have certain drills and exercises to go through, which is their only occupation. They amuse themselves with pigeons and birds, almost every man carrying a bird about with him on a stick, or in a cage, and they have flocks of pigeons with whistles attached to them, so that when they fly through the air the whistles sound. I speak from experience when I add that if a foreigner should try to use a camera in the streets of Peking, he will

find this idle population his worst enemy. Pigeons, birds and everything is forgotten for the moment and a most unmanageable mob is
the result.

The south gate of the palace faces the Ch'ien-men, the central south
gate of the Tartar City and is approached by a series of immense paved
courtyards, divided one from another by massive gateways, above
which rise imposing pavilions with yellow tiled overhanging roofs,
flanked by great towers built in the same style and similarly roofed
with Imperial yellow. The outer south gate of all palaces and houses is
a place of honour and importance: in the Imperial Palace it is called
the Ta-Ch'ing-men, which seems to be a high-sounding title capable of
various meanings, as 'Front Gate', 'Gate of the Dynasty', and it is also
named the 'Great Pure Gate'. It is by this gate only that the Emperor
enters or leaves his residence. Having passed this, you are within the
walls of the palace, and then come a succession of gates and halls of a
very celestial character, if we may judge by their names. The first is the
T'ien-an-men or 'Gate of Heavenly Peace'; then follows the Lu-an-
men or 'Gate of Order'; after that the Wu-men or 'Gate of the Midday
Sun'.

Walking from the Wu-men, the gate on the south side, courtyard
after courtyard with their great halls and temples are passed. The first
is the T'ai-Ho-Men ('Gate of Great Felicity'), in the courtyard of which
stands the famous hall, T'ai-Ho-Tien ('Hall of Great Felicity'); further
north comes the middle temple called Chung-Ho-Tien, then the Pao-
Ho-Tien and after this courtyard there is the Ch'ien-Ch'ing-Men
('Gate of Steadfast Purity'), in the adjoining courtyard of which stands
the Throne Hall called the Ch'ien-Ch'ing-Kung ('Palace of Steadfast
Purity') in which the Prince Regent[43] receives the diplomats in state
audience. Ministers are now carried in sedan chairs from the Ta-
Ch'ing-Men where they take a short rest in the Shang-Shu-Fang
library or building of study for young Princes of the Blood: (in private
audience the Prince Regent receives generally in the hall Yang-Hsin-
Tien). And here are the apartments occupied by the Emperor, where
he sits enthroned receiving the homage and obeisance of his court on
certain great state occasions. There he sits on the Chinese New Year's
Day, on his own birthday, and when conferring great literary degrees.
Also at various other times prescribed by the rigid ceremonial of which
he is the slave.

The Emperor's 'bulwark' [42]

---

[42] The appearance of a pigtail on one of these soldiers suggests that the slide features a
Chinese military unit: such units supported the Ch'ing dynasty in addition to Manchu
troops.

[43] In 1908 both the Empress Dowager Ci Xi and the imprisoned Emperor Guangxu died
within a day or two of each other. As the newly enthroned Emperor P'u-Yi was only a little
boy, his father Prince Chun was named regent to act on the Emperor's behalf. This situation
lasted until the abdication of P'u-Yi in February 1912, nine months before James
Hutchinson's departure from China.

He is placed apart, and exists under conditions which separate his life and fate from that of all human beings on earth. Everything he does and the conduct of everyone about him is rigidly defined in a Book of Ceremonies. Every event in his life from his birth to his death is regulated by this authority, which is said to extend to as much as 200 volumes. Like some god surrounded by the celestial hosts, throned in dignity and thus secluded from contact with the powers of evil, the deified Emperor of China, encircled by his protecting army of Manchus, seems defended against all outward danger or influence from his enemies. The abstract and mythical ideas of old are repeated in this sacred monarch, who in his secluded position is said to be 'Lonely as a god'. The ancestral tablets of the deceased emperors of the dynasty are placed together with those of the deity in the Temple of Heaven, making them as it were the equals of God, with whom they are worshipped. That this palace should be looked upon as a sort of celestial abode, or third heaven, is what one might expect from the conditions of the case, and the high-sounding names given to each part of it proves that such is the case.

Experiences of the streets of Peking, or of its pig-tailed Tartar population[44], would not be likely to suggest that the one was planned or the other organised from anything that could be called a heavenly model. But the description just given will show that the capital city of the Celestials is not without a design, and that, too, seemingly of a very ancient symbolical character pointing to the old idea of the visible and the invisible Jerusalems.

The Temple of Heaven

There are said to be three different religions in China – the Taoist, the Confucian and the Buddhist – but the state worship which is performed at the Temple of Heaven in Peking is entirely different from any of these forms of faith. These three forms of religion are not ignored by the state, but that which is practised at Peking is the real state religion, and has no resemblance to any state religion elsewhere. It is confined to the capital and the Emperor is the only priest. It is an Imperial worship, with a deified monarch at its head.

The Temple of Heaven is situated in the southern section of the Chinese City and is the most sacred temple of the capital. This temple was originally erected by Emperor Yung-Lo (AD 1421) of the Ming dynasty and was enlarged by Ch'ien-Lung in 1751. It has a wall enclosure running around it which is three and a half miles in length, and the whole area is divided up into many large compounds which

---

[44] Bosworth observes that this is a misnomer, if Hutchinson was equating 'Tartar' with 'Manchu'. Only Chinese men were forced to grow pigtails, a sign of subservience to Manchu rulers.

have large and splendid lawns and beautifully wooded grounds. The temple edifices are the Ch'i-Nien-Tien, the Huang-Ch'iung-Yu and the Pai-T'ai. The Ch'i-Nien-Tien is the tallest of the buildings, being cone-shaped in form with three pagoda-like roofs. On the top is a large golden button which is visible from a great distance. When walking on the south wall of the Tartar City this large building can be seen most plainly and also when passing from Feng-T'ai Station to the Ch'ien-Men terminus of the Imperial Railway of North China, it is easily pointed out from the carriage window, especially with the morning sun shining on the glazed tile roofs. The roof tiles of this building are of a peculiar dark blue glazed earthenware and they attract the eye just as much as the golden button on the top. This building is of most interesting Chinese architecture and contains tablets to the memory of all the Emperors who reigned over China, from Shun-Chi (1644–1662) up to Kwang-Hsu (1875–1908).

The second building, the Huang-Ch'iung-Yu, is of a similar construction but is not so tall, and with the exception of idols there is nothing of importance concerning it.

I and some other visitors managed to find our way into this Temple of Heaven. There is no known prohibition against strangers going in, but it is not the custom for people to do so, and there are no recognized arrangements for admittance. The chances of anyone making good an entrance depends on his power of jumping over high walls, making a rush at a door and forcing himself inside. These operations, combined with the magic influence of pieces of silver, called 'dollars' which are in use hereabouts, generally accomplish the object. Our party got over the first wall and jumping down on the other side, we found ourselves in what seemed to be an extensive park, with avenues of trees. No one was to be seen, so we walked to what appeared to be the second wall, and made for the nearest door, but found it all too strong for us, and the dollar influence could not be tested for the absence of anyone to try it on. We then turned to the left and walked cautiously towards another gateway, close to a house, at the door of which we saw two men. An open wicket door was also to be seen, which we approached stealthily, and at last by a run were masters of the position. The two men made an effort to stop us but were too late. Putting us out again did not seem to enter their heads; on the contrary, some slight allusion to a dollar caused one of them to come as our guide, for there was still a third wall. Whether the coincidence be intentional or not I cannot say, but the palace in Peking is also enclosed within a triple wall. There is a wall round the palace; a second wall encloses the Imperial City; the Tartar City is outside that again and the whole is enclosed by the great wall of Peking. The palace, like the Temple of Heaven, and indeed all temples, palaces and public buildings in China, faces due south. The Ch'ien-men or south gate previously mentioned is in a direct line south, from the palace gate to the street leading to the Temple of Heaven, and it is through this gate that the Emperor goes out, to sacrifice in the Temple of Heaven. All this is, no doubt, part of one plan, probably astronomical, or possibly astrological, for astrology has to do with many things in China.

Within the second wall we had on our right the Hall of Penitential Fasting, which is a large square of buildings, with moat, bridges and walls around it. Our guide led to the left through the park, and then through a thick wood of old cypress trees which seemed to surround the whole of the temple and extends as far as the south altar. Like the temples of old it is literally in a grove. We were seeking for a large temple and could not see it, so completely was it hid by this dark, dense wood of ancient trees. The effect of this was all lost on our party, who were trying to see where the gate could be found, and to take advantage of it should it be open. At last I saw the head of our column make a rush; I followed and found myself within the third wall, and the Temple of Heaven stood before me. This was the north altar and we lost no time, for there was yet the chance, not to be thrown away, of seeing the inside; so another rush soon took us up the three flights of steps, across the top of the terrace, and to our great satisfaction the door was open. Our sudden appearance in the very centre of this vast place seemed to have taken everyone by surprise. A man of pig-tail nationality soon made his appearance and began scolding very loudly, not only at us but at the pig-tailed individuals around. The man who had come with us from the other door said nothing, for he was held under the magic spell of baksheesh. The potency of this began to work upon them all except our scolding friend, who took to shutting the doors, but before he did I managed to get a photograph of the interior and another of the roof.

The great Temple of Heaven

Although standing on such an elaborate superstructure of marble, the building, like almost all buildings hereabouts, is of wood. Four very high round pillars support the central and highest roof, which is nearly all gilt on the inside. Twelve smaller columns sustain the second roof, which reaches only from the four outside pillars, thus leaving visible from within the whole height of the highest roof. Twelve still smaller wooden columns from the outer circle support the lowest roof which, like the second, only roofs the space between the pillars which sustain it and the circle of pillars next to them. All this woodwork is elaborately painted and gilt.

The tiles on the roof are all of a dark blue glazed earthenware. The altar to God is on the north, and the altars to the eight deceased Emperors are on the east and west. It was all very dirty and dusty, and on the outside grass and weeds were growing through the joints in the marble.

We got on the great paved way which connects the two altars near its middle, and walked to the south altar. This altar, the third building or edifice of which I have told you, the Pai T'ai, stands in the open. It is of immense dimensions, 210 feet across at its base, and built of white marble. Its top can be reached by ascending three flights of steps, one from each of the cardinal points; these stairs have three divisions of nine steps each. The whole is surrounded by a low wall with open marble gateways on each side, facing the four ascents. The wall is square in plan, and in the south east corner is the furnace or altar for burning the bullock, with eight other altars, smaller and of iron, where offerings to the eight deceased ancestors are also burned. The four ascents, with approaches and gates to the four cardinal points, suggest that an astro-geographical meaning was intended. Most of the Imperial temples of Peking have been constructed with references to the relation of numbers, and this is particularly marked in the Temple of Heaven. The number 9 figures very largely in it. The ascent to each terrace has nine steps, the whole ascent being $3 \times 9 = 27$. The pavement on the circular top is formed by nine circles of marble slabs, the second is formed by eighteen, the third of twenty-seven, and so on, each circle being a multiple of nine, until at the outer circle it is $9 \times 9 = 81$ – a favourite number in Chinese philosophy. Most travellers describe the north altar as the 'Temple of Heaven' but in reality it is only a part of it. It is particularly imposing to a visitor from its having a permanent building on the top platform. The circular triple terrace of white marble is the same here as at the 'South Altar', with the difference that there are eight ascents instead of four.

The function of Imperial worship in the Temple of Heaven is one of the great sights of Peking. The Emperor in going to worship heaven is accompanied by hundreds of the highest officials of state. They all

The Temple of Heaven's ornate wooden ceiling

One of the processional sedan chairs

appear in gorgeous silk dresses and uniforms of state. With them are hundreds of officials of lower ranks, also a multitude of servants, besides thousands of soldiers in the cortège.

The Emperor comes to the place the night before, being carried, accompanied by the highest officials, in very elaborate sedan chairs and escorted by the cortège just mentioned, the whole forming a very elaborate procession. He spends the night in the Hall of Penitential Fasting – the name indicating the character of this part of the proceedings.

This is in a separate section in the Temple of Heaven grounds, a separate enclosure from the altars and surrounded by a moat, the top of which is ornamented with marble railings and marble bridges: inside the square moat are several buildings. The Emperor stays here, rests overnight in preparation for worship and the guide who takes you round generally brings you to this so-called Chai Kung and shows you the Imperial Chair. It is situated in the main building, or at least what appeared to me to be so. This chair is carved out of solid oak and is a truly marvellous piece of Chinese architecture. The ceremonies carried out at the Temple of Heaven are very elaborate, and no doubt this Imperial Chair is an important addition to that part performed in the Hall of Penitential Fasting.

Emperors for a flash! Three Inniskillings on the Emperor's chair

The Emperor is a divine ruler whose acts are the 'Will of Heaven' and who announces them to heaven and earth, and to all under heaven. Even the dead are informed as to what he is doing. The grand oriental idea of being supreme over everything is assumed and acted on. He is a priest as well as a king. No-one dare approach him without the most abject homage: prostrations due only to a god are exacted in his presence. He is surrounded by soothsayers, concubines and eunuchs. His place is a Celestial city in itself.

It was something to have been in the midst of this, and to have got even stolen glimpses of such a strange state of things. It was like getting an actual peep back into the most ancient times, and seeing with one's own eyes what is only read of in books. What struck me most about the Temple of Heaven is that there are no images anywhere to suggest the slightest ideas of idolatry: perhaps the Emperor himself is the only god worshipped. So free is it from statues or pictures that a Mahomedan or Presbyterian might use it as a place of worship.

The Emperor visits the Temple of Heaven during the first moon of each Chinese year, when he worships before the ancestral tablets in the large temple, Ch'i-Nien-Tien. Here he gets his annual mission as ruler. During the fourth moon of the Chinese calendar, he comes to worship in the smaller temple, the Huang-Ch'iung-Yu, where he prays for a good harvest and rain. His third visit is made in the eleventh moon when he worships at the open altar.

It is the yearly custom for the Emperor to read at the Temple of Heaven a list of all criminals executed during the past twelve months, and to pray that if any of them have been wrongfully punished, their sins may not be visited upon them in the next world. On this occasion the Emperor lays aside his robes of state, appears as a criminal himself, and as such walks from the Hall of Penitential Fasting.

Ascending the throne

The ceremonial when an Emperor ascends the throne in China is, as might be supposed, a most elaborate affair, and no doubt figures largely in those 200 volumes which guide every detail of Imperial existence. Wishing to know how the programme in that country resembled a European coronation, I made various enquiries, the result of which will show that there is little or no resemblance between them. As usual, the Astronomical Board – sort of Enquiring-into-the-Heavens officials – have to interrogate the heavens, not only for an auspicious day, but for the particular fortunate moment; and when this has come, the first step is the presentation of a petition to the Emperor, asking him to ascend the throne. This is, no doubt, a mere form but it would be interesting to know who it is who assumes the right thus to petition, because it seems to imply a liberty of questioning his right to ascend the throne. The event is then proclaimed, and the proclamation, announcing it to the whole Empire, figures largely in the ceremonies.

The phoenix is as important a heraldic figure in China as the dragon. It belongs to the Imperial insignia, and on this occasion a phoenix of gold appears with the proclamation hanging to its beak. The Emperor first worships at the temple of his ancestors[45]; after which the officer of the Astronomical Board announces that the auspicious moment has arrived. The Emperor then ascends to a golden chariot; elephants and guards are in attendance, and the members of the Board of Rites are also here to guide every movement. When the procession reaches the great hall, the president of the Board of Rites kneels and prays the Emperor to assume the sway. This he does, sitting with his face towards the south. Gongs and music now sound through the hall, and the whole court fall on their knees and perform the *kow-tow* – that is, they strike their foreheads nine times on the ground.

He is now Emperor, or 'Viceregent of all under Heaven', and worshipped as such. The accomplished event then has to be declared to the universe, and the proclamation is consequently taken from the beak of the phoenix. The Imperial Seal, which had been placed on a table, is applied to the proclamation, and the President of the Board of Rites comes forward, and kneeling receives it in a golden vase. The Emperor has now finished his part of the ceremony and retires on his golden chariot to his private apartments in the palace. The proclamation is next taken to a raised platform from which it is read, everyone kneeling all the time. It is then returned to the golden vase, and carried back to the golden phoenix, from whose bill it is again suspended. It is afterwards copied and sent to all parts of the Empire. That is a very slight sketch of the ceremony, but I believe it contains the main features of what takes place. There is no anointing oil, or placing of a crown on the head, and indeed scarcely any point to give it a resemblance to our coronation ceremonies. Here we have a bird – the phoenix – a sort of celestial creature, a messenger from heaven, bearing the proclamation or declaration that the 'Son of Heaven' is to reign.

When an Emperor of China dies and departs on 'The Great Journey', he 'ascends on the dragon, to be a guest on high': such is the official language in which the fact of his death is announced to foreign Ministers and throughout the Empire. When a new Emperor mounts the throne, the phoenix comes from above to proclaim his advent. This close and constant intercommunication with the next world may seem strange to Europeans, but we see how familiar it is to the people of this country. We boast of our railways and our facilities for travelling from one country to another; but here when an Emperor of China dies the great dragon performs the part of a special train to heaven. We cannot telegraph beyond the limits of this small globe of ours; but here when a new Emperor comes to the throne the phoenix appears with the

The phoenix: the messenger from Heaven which proclaimed new Emperors

The dragon which was said to carry a dead Emperor to Heaven

[45] (in the Imperial City).

latest telegraphic despatch, or official document from 'on High', containing the appointment. There is even a banking or money order-office system between this world and the next. Deceased ancestors seem to be very poor, or in the regions which they inhabit perhaps the prices of everything may have gone up of late, for large remittances have to be continually sent. Everywhere we can see paper imitations of silver and gold, which are cast in ingots in the form of an ancient shoe. The imitations look exactly like the ingots. By burning a number of these at an ancestral tablet an equivalent sum is transmitted to the defunct individual. There must be a very large quantity of these paper shoes used if one may judge from the supply visible in the shops. The bullock which is burned at the winter solstice at the Temple of Heaven is supposed to ascend to the celestial regions. And, if I mistake not, the Chinese believe this of all sacrifices which are consumed by fire.

Other temples and sights of Peking

The Temple of Agriculture is situated on the south-west end of the Ch'ien-Men Road and in front of the Temple of Heaven: its area is rather smaller and it is of inferior grandeur. The large building, which is called Tai-Shui-Tien, is nonetheless of fine Chinese architecture. The principal ceremony at this temple takes place in the Spring when the Emperor ploughs a piece of ground and sows in it the seeds of one or two kinds of grain. He does this as an example of husbandry and industry to all his subjects, and a very good and worthy example it is from a monarch to his people. It may be worth noting that this ceremony has reference to the ancient history of Buddha: for we are told that Soddhodana, King of Kapila, and father of Buddha, celebrated the festival of Commencement of Sowing-time; with Brahmins and nobles and 199 ploughs they broke the earth and sowed the first seeds. This is important as showing that the particular Imperial religious festivals performed at Peking were not at former periods isolated in that corner of the world. There are interesting implements of agriculture kept in one of the side buildings and for a small tip the temple keepers will take you there and show you the ploughs and husbandman's hat and clothes which the Emperor wears.

The Chinese plough

The Chinese are certainly good agriculturists. I have heard them much praised in this respect, but whether their high efficiency is the result of following the model set by their Emperor or not I cannot pretend to say. A more detailed account of these temples and all the ceremonies performed, and likewise further particulars of the other Imperial temples in Peking, would be a valuable addition to our information. My stay in Peking was too short to let me do much. It would take one a long time to study the various temples in and around the capital. I have to thank my guide and interpreter, in addition to

Returning from market

other residents there, for the information obtained in connection with the various forms of religion and worship.

So far I have only touched on what we might call 'State Worship', which is entirely different from the real forms of Buddhist worship as adopted in these parts. Peking is the place for this state worship, and most of the temples there are connected with it. State worship is more or less the ancient ancestral religion, which is Tomb-worship. This they trace back to the symbolic signification of the *Yin-Yang* and the *Pa Kua*, two separate forms of the dual powers of nature (masculine and feminine) and which are now beginning to be understood as the basis on which all the ancient religions of the world are founded.

I visited various temples in Peking and found none of them to resemble the Temple of Heaven, in that they all exhibited numerous idols of every description. Perhaps a slight description of a few of these temples will give one a fair idea of the general construction of all Buddhist temples in China, or at least those around the capital; which must not be taken into consideration with the ordinary temples or 'joss houses' that one finds in the smaller cities and in the interior. 'Temple' is the general name of all the Chinese places of worship. Red walls imply that the temple was founded by Imperial sanction. The Taoist temples are occasionally occupied by Buddhist priests, having passed into their hands by sale or by the expulsion of the Taoists. One class of these are always monasteries, and others are classed as spiritual shrines of Emperors, of Confucius and other deceased worthies. All temples of no matter what denomination must exhibit on the altar a tablet inscribed with the words Wan-Wan-Sui-Yeh, which means Lord of ten thousand times ten thousand years: i.e. the Emperor, as a proof that religious convictions are not allowed to interfere with political fidelity. Buddhist priests shave the entire head. Taoist priests or monks do not. The pleasant occupation of visiting the different temples takes several days.

The Yellow Temple

The Yellow Temple situated a short distance outside the city receives its title from its colour. All temples about the capital have yellow roofs but during the ages the yellow has turned black, this however being rather an exception which makes it so noticeable in this respect. There are a number of temple buildings here enclosed in a large compound and divided into two separate sections. The eastern section is in a better state of preservation: here we see a number of large temple buildings which were built during the times of the Emperor Ch'ien-Lung (AD 1736–1796). The western section is almost entirely in ruins but here stands the most striking feature of this temple, also made during the reign of Ch'ien-Lung, a large marble monument dedicated to the life of the great 'Dalai Lama'. Around the monument itself are demonstrated a series of Lama functions, all of which are either carved into the stone or are in relief. Unfortunately vandalism is observed as many heads of the relief figures are cut off. I did not see any forms of worship going on in this temple when I visited it. In fact the place seemed to be deserted, with the exception of about half-a-dozen old priests who seemed to be in charge of the place.

The Pao-Kuo-Ssu is located in the west of the Chinese City near the Kuang-An-Men. It is supposed to be one of the most ancient of the great number of temples which are located in and around Peking. This temple is dedicated to Kwan-Yin or Goddess of Mercy and has in its interior hundreds of images of all descriptions. When our little party arrived at this temple we thought, at first, that any chance of getting into the buildings was hopeless. Our interpreter and guide on this occasion was a native Christian who volunteered to come with us. He soon found one of pig-tail nationality whom he put under the magic spell of a dollar at once, when all the doors to our satisfaction were unlocked. Our presence in this sacred place soon collected a crowd,

The figure of Kwan-Yin, the Chinese
Goddess of Mercy

from whence they come I do not know. I took it that they were all under
the magic spell of baksheesh. It is so in all these places and I believe that
most of those around, especially the priests, exist almost on donations
given by foreigners who visit these places. From the appearance of the
place one could easily imagine that the founder had the same idea in
his mind. Each apartment – and there are many – is securely locked
and the old priest who accompanies one round carries a large bundle of
keys, just as curious looking as the locks which they are
intended to open. Before each lock in turn is opened a ten
cent piece must be given, the whole of which realises enough
to keep him and his partnership for a considerable period.

The most striking feature about the interior of nearly
every compartment was the number of huge idols. The
Chinese have a god to help them in nearly every need in life,
hence they get a good collection. No doubt they look very
real – in fact one could imagine at times that they had life.
Wishing to know the names, or at least the sort of need that
each of those huge individuals were supposed to supply, I
made enquiries and the following are some of the names
given to me: 'God of Long Life', 'God of Riches', 'God of
Peace', 'God of War', 'Goddess of Mercy', 'Goddess of
Children' etc, all of which will give a fair idea of the
superstitions of all those who worship them. The principal
idols are erected on very elaborate platforms and draped
with some sort of silk looking material. In front are placed
five vessels, generally of bronze: that in the centre is for
incense, which is presented by the worshipper in the form
of what is known as 'joss sticks'. These are simply long
pastilles, which burn for a certain length of time, and in the
flowery language of China are called 'the fragrance of an
hour'. The two vessels on each side of this are candlesticks,

The God of Riches

and those at each end are for flowers. In addition to the gods, there are
a large number of smaller images, called disciples.

A respectful Corporal Hutchinson
amongst the Gods of Work

The Temple of the East Mountain is another very interesting place. What struck me here at first sight was the huge incense burner in front of the main building. This I afterwards discovered was used as a sort of Post Office to the next world, for it is here that the gold and silver ingot shoes and counterfeit money is burned, in order to transmit an equivalent sum to the dead ancestors.

This is a Taoist temple in which people worship the sacred T'ai-Shan, a mountain in the east of Shan-Tung Province. In the main room we were shown where the Emperor sleeps, should he stay overnight in preparation for worship. It was in this temple I discovered to my

The Temple of the East Mountain[46] with its incense burner

46   This temple was known as the Tung-Yueh-Miao (in the Wade-Giles spelling).

own satisfaction that presents were brought and offered to the gods in return for some blessing received. Adjoining the Emperor's room is the principal temple, where a very large idol is situated, a huge structure of very elaborate finish. Under the idol is a large chest of drawers. People coming to worship this idol as a rule bring it a present which is placed in this chest. When I visited there I pulled out one of the drawers and found to my surprise a huge pair of Chinese shoes placed in it. The idol being very large, it got presented with a pair of shoes accordingly, so that if it wanted to go out it could wear them. Of course this appears ridiculous to us, but it is their belief and if you laughed at the idea of it, they would appear greatly annoyed. In front of this large image stands an incense burner containing a small smouldering light, which is supposed to never go out.

The Temple of the Eighteen Hells

Leaving this temple, about five minutes walk brings us to the Temple of the Eighteen Hells or punishments. In this temple are demonstrated various punishments which are supposed to be awarded after death for sins committed in this world and one is confronted with some ghastly sights. There is another room, close to the punishment room, where a person who has committed a sin can sit for a certain number of days without food or drink so as to atone for their sins and therefore escape the punishments of the Eighteen Hells. The greater the sin, the longer they have to sit and starve. All these things prove to us how superstitious are the forms of their heathen religion. This temple is much smaller than the Temple of the East Mountain.

The Two Princes of the Eighteen Punishments

On each side of the entrance to nearly every temple stands a very huge vicious looking idol. These are called gate idols and are placed there to guard the building from evil spirits. The Chinese are very superstitious as regards evil spirits and every precaution is taken to frighten or keep them away, for in their estimation the presence of an evil spirit would destroy the sacredness of the place and make the gods very angry. And further on are the four heavenly kings, who sit there to guard the place from evil demons. The first shrine contains images of the three Precious Ones, the Buddhist past, present and to come, otherwise known as the 'Buddhist Trinity'. The second contains a pagoda which covers some relic of Buddha. And the last contains the figure of Kwan-Yin, the Chinese goddess of mercy.

The Confucian temples are to be found in every prefectural and district city, and in every market town throughout the empire. Their walls are generally red, which was the official colour under the Chou Dynasty. They contain commemorative tablets of Confucius and of a large number of scholars of later ages whose writings have tended towards elucidating or disseminating the teachings of the Great Sage.

The sacred rites connected with temples have always much interested me. I was quartered for six months in a temple compound, on the Wei-Hai-Wei frontier during the recent rebellion. And it was here that I gained a fairly good insight into the forms of ceremony as carried out at such places. The Chinese month is taken from the moon, a new moon commencing a new month. It was on the first and fifteenth of every month that the principal ceremonies took place at this temple. On the night previous to a ceremony taking place, the old priest who was in charge had to ensure that the gods were awake and prepared to receive worship the following morning. This little ceremony of waking

A gate idol

One of the Four Heavenly Kings

up the gods meant a restless night on the priest's part, and indeed a restless night to us who were sleeping within the compound. About 9 p.m. this ceremony generally commenced, when the priest lighted the show up with about twenty Chinese lanterns. Incense was then placed in front of each god and lighted. The next part of the ceremony I took to be the real awaking. A large bell in the compound is first struck a few times, after which gongs, drums and bells sound through the building creating a terrible noise. For this last part the priest's family assist. We got so familiar with the old priest, that very often a helping hand was given on our behalf to assist him.

About 4 a.m. the pilgrims arrived to the tune of their village band – a definition given by us! Each pilgrim, as he arrives, places incense in front of each god in turn, then bows before it, touching his head to the ground three times. The transmitting of money to deceased ancestors then takes place. A large brick incense burner figures highly in this ceremony. Every pilgrim visiting the temple brings with him a quantity of gold and silver paper money which is burned in this brick arrangement. This part of the ceremony shows clearly the crafty and miserly nature of this people. They offer to their gods and ancestors counterfeit money, pasteboard dollars covered with tinfoil resembling silver and gold. A Chinaman prides himself on making an offering to his god or his ancestor of several thousand dollars, which cost him only a trifle. He will fairly chuckle over the thought that his stupid god or his dead ancestor, not knowing the difference between false coins and true, will give him credit for the full amount in good money.

A temple in ruins is a most striking place. I visited one in Peking and found that its decay was great: but the most striking feature was the condition of the gods. 'Out at elbows' could be literally applied to many of them, for the wooden framework could in many cases be seen projecting from that particular joint. The priests of this temple, I was told, were using every effort to excite charity in order to get enough money for the restoration of this temple. They went about begging in the most pitiful manner, going under any pain which in their ideas would excite the necessary charity for obtaining funds for this pious purpose. Gods do get out of repair in countries where even no visible presentations of them are made – at least in men's minds they do; but when there is a material and visible construction, which gets out of order and gets daily the worse for the wear, they make a very melancholy exhibition. They have a foolish look – all the more foolish because we remember that they have been gods, and have received worship. It is rather sorrowful to find that a god's existence depends upon the strength of joints, mortices, and pegs of wood; and here we see that divine beauty, where it is represented by putty, paint and gold leaf, may all fall off and leave nothing but ghastliness visible. The only thing that I could find about the whole place which had the slightest approach to the divine was the old priest in charge, who begged us in such sorrowful way for a donation that I think one of our party gave him a dollar. This no doubt will assist in paying for a little repairs to one of those ghastly looking structures. One could have wished that those priests' time and patience had been devoted to some more worthy object than that of re-carpentering 'gods out of repair'.

Situated on the southern section of the east wall of the Tartar City wall is a very historic observatory. This wonderful observatory was erected during the Yuan dynasty and under Kublai-Khan (AD 1279) It is the first observatory of which the world has record[47]. Here we still see some of the old instruments which have been in use for ages. In 1900 a part of these historic instruments were taken to Europe. It is stated that the Chinese afterwards made a present of them to Germany and France[48]. Several duplicates have replaced the genuine ones. Most of the instruments standing in the tower were executed during the 17th century, under the care of the Jesuit Father

Not a stately pleasure-dome but an observatory, decreed under Kublai Khan

---

[47] This assertion is probably not true: the *Guinness Book of Records* states that 'The oldest observatory building extant is the 'Tower of the Winds' used by Andronichus of Cyrrhus in Athens, Greece *c.*100 BC.'

[48] In fact the original instruments were taken by France and Germany as spoils from the Boxer War. Germany was obliged to return its share by the terms of the Versailles Treaty following World War 1.

Bronze globe at the historic Chinese
Observatory

Verbiest[49]. It may be said that the historic observatory gave great influence to the Jesuit Fathers who first settled in China. Beautiful dragon-adorned instruments of bronze were presented by the Jesuits and King Louis of France. In the courtyard below the tower is still one of the old instruments which was made over 500 hundred years ago.

To get to the western section of the Tartar City we must follow a zig-zag of narrow streets, from the Ch'ien-Men Gate until finally the main street running from the Shun-Chi-Men Gate to the north is reached. This part of the Manchu City contains a large populace of Mahomedan families. Peking contains in all about fifteen thousand Mahomedan families.

Another place of interest in Peking is the Zoological and Botanical Gardens, termed the experimental station. This pretty spot is situated about two miles outside the city[50], from the Hsi-Chi-Men or northwest gate along the west wall of Peking. It is an entirely new enterprise, founded by the mandarin Cheng Chang, a vice-president of the Department of Commerce and Agriculture. As one enters, one is struck with wonderment at the great stretch of agricultural land which covers an area of several square miles. There are large artistic flower beds, small lakes, fine tea houses and other buildings. One can enjoy a boat trip on the lake, and rickshaws and sedan chairs can be hired. In the height of the summer the ponds are covered with lotus which make an enchanting picture. In the north-western section of the park a several storied building has been erected in

The entrance to Peking's Botanical and
Zoological Gardens

[49] From the *New Advent Catholic Encyclopedia:* Father Ferdinand Verbiest SJ, 'missionary and astronomer, b. at Pitthem near Courtrai, Belgium, 9 Oct., 1623; d. at Peking, 28 January, 1688. He entered the Society of Jesus on 2 Sept., 1641 . . . In 1658 with thirty-five new missionaries he accompanied Father Martin Martini on his return to China . . .'.
[50] Where it remains to this day.

European style which was intended to serve as a visiting and resting place for the Imperial Family. Near the south-western section there is a museum where agricultural experiments are shown. Here one can see the different stages of silk industry, from the worm to the butterfly, including eggs, cocoons and the spinning of the silk threads.

In the zoological section one is able to spend a very interesting afternoon. There are huge aviaries of hundreds of species of birds, from the ostrich down to a little bird which is about the size of a large bumble-bee. Also a good collection of animals, the largest being the huge carcass of the elephant and the smallest animal is the beaver. One is also struck with the huge aquariums containing many kinds of fish, some of them having a very ugly appearance.

5 *Manners and customs of the Chinese*

WE call the Chinese heathens. They look upon us as little better than savages. They think we are very impolite and pity us because we do not dress, act and live as they do. When two Europeans meet they clasp hands. When two Chinese friends come together, they shake their own fists at each other, and if they are going in the same direction they walk off in single file like geese. We cut our finger nails short. The Chinese let theirs grow long, and long nails are with them the sign of a lady or gentleman. All those who do not work with their hands are proud of their nails. Scholars, officials, doctors and other professional men often have nails from one to six inches long. Ladies sometimes have silver shields which they put over their nails to keep them from breaking. I once saw a Chinese merchant who could rest the palm of his hand upon his chin and scratch the back of his neck with his nails.

A family group in their winter clothes

The Chinese do not kiss. They seldom embrace and in bowing to one another they bend down almost to the ground. We take off our hats when we enter a house. The Chinese gentleman keeps his hat on. We ask first after the wives and daughters of our friends. The Chinese would consider such questions an insult. And the girls of a family remain out of the room when gentlemen call on their father or brothers. The Chinese girls are not courted. Marriages are made by parents through professional matchmakers, and a husband seldom sees his wife until he is married. The wife is the slave of her mother-in-law, who has the right to whip her if she does not obey.

In China the men wear the finest embroidery and the high officials have their hats decorated with feathers and wear strings of beads around their necks. The men often wear bracelets and gentlemen are fond of long stockings, while their wives go about in short socks. The Chinese women often wear pantaloons above which there is a sack coming half way down to the knees. The men in full dress wear gowns which reach from their necks to their feet. A Chinese gentleman's shoes are usually of cloth. Ours are of leather and we black them all over, but he whitens only the sides of the soles.

Some of our women have the bad habit of squeezing their waists by lacing, and some Europeans consider a small waist a mark of beauty. The Chinese women are proud of small feet, and they bind the heel down into the foot by tying the four small toes under it so that their feet are much like the ends of clubs. The binding often begins when the girls are three years of age. The bandages are kept on from that time until death, except when they are removed for washing the feet. The compression causes terrible pain and the bandage is sometimes so tight that the foot breaks in two at the instep, the bones coming through the flesh.

We wear black when we go into mourning. The Chinese at such times wear white and they send out mourning cards which are printed on white paper, though ordinarily the colour of their visiting cards is the brightest red. After the time of mourning has half passed away, they send out other cards upon which is printed 'Grief is not so bitter as before'. They put on a garb of light blue for half-mourning, and when the days of their mourning are ended, they give feast to their friends.

The Chinese begin their books at the back instead of the front and in dating their letters they put the year first, then the month (or moon) and then the day.

They have many queer kinds of food: they boil their bread instead of baking it, and in N. China we meet many cook pedlars who are selling boiled biscuits. The Chinese are fond of an expensive soup made of 'birds' nests'. They eat eggs but never serve them soft-boiled; they pickle their eggs in lime and the older such eggs are, the better they like them. They never drink cold water and their wine is served piping hot. They have their tea served very weak with neither milk nor sugar. One of the chief meats sold is pork: we shall see black hogs all over China. They trot through the streets and wallow in the puddles by the sides of the road. They seem to us the dirtiest hogs in the world, but the Chinese think that there is no meat more delicious than pork. Cats, dogs and rats are sometimes sold and eaten in the poorer parts of the cities: black cats and dogs are considered the best.

The Chinese have theatres but the performances are carried on during the day-time, and instead of lemonade &c they have themselves

A well-to-do Manchu lady, seated right, with a Chinese woman, possibly her personal attendant. Note the smaller, bound feet of the Chinese

Selling boiled bread

A typical street theatre

Musicians busking outside the Yi-Wei
Woodworking Factory

Coolie having a meal[51]

Gambling with a street hawker

served with tea, watermelon and pumpkin seeds at which they sup and nibble while the acting goes on.

They seldom wash the whole body, and it is said that many Chinamen receive only two baths while on earth, one at birth and the other when prepared for the coffin. They do not wash their hands before dinner, but a servant brings a hot wet cloth to the guests at the table and they rub off their hands and faces with this, passing it from one to another. The Chinese eat from tables as we do, but they use chopsticks and not forks to convey the food to their mouths. The food is served in small porcelain bowls, the meat being cut into little cubes, and the tea is served in cups with the saucer on top.

The Chinese baby has no cradle, the little one is strapped to the back of its mother or that of a servant. If the mother is a working woman she goes about her business with the baby tied to her back. When the baby begins to talk it is given a pair of knit shoes, with a cat's face on the toes, this being supposed to render it as sure-footed as a cat.

The Chinese are great gamblers, they even gamble for their daily food. Cockfighting and quail fighting are common and in some of the cities we see men kneeling down on the streets about little bowls in which fighting crickets are placed: the little insects are urged on to fight by being tickled with straws and they fight until they are dead. A good fighting cricket is valuable, high bets being made upon the results of such contests.

One of the most striking features of China is the terrible poverty of the lower classes of the people. Beggars exist everywhere in large numbers. Children are sometimes stolen and made blind in order that they may beg more successfully. The beggars of each city, as a rule, have unions or clubs to which they all belong. They divide the city into sections, each member having his own street or block. These beggars will undergo any pain in order to excite pity. I once saw a half-naked man whose clothes consisted of a strip of coffee sacking wrapped about his hips. He sat on the stones with the two raw stumps of his legs stretched out before him and his feet which he had cut off to excite pity were lying by his side.

The Chinese can live more cheaply than any other people of the world, and we are surprised at the saving which we see everywhere. Nothing goes to waste. The straw and the weeds and even the leaves of the trees are gathered for fuel. Clothing rather than fire is used to keep out the cold. Fuel costs so much that the poor man never builds a fire if he can help it. A large part of his diet is rice, which is cooked in quantities and re-warmed for breakfast by pouring hot water over it.

[51] It may be that this photo should not be credited to Hutchinson, having also featured – unattributed – with the caption 'Selling Jellied Bean Curd' in a book entitled '*Old Photos of Beijing*', Lin Wenbi and Xu Dongsheng, Renmin Meishu Chuban She (People's Fine Arts Publishing House), Beijing, 1989.

The hot water used at such times and for tea is often bought from hot water pedlars at about 1 cash per bucket-full. At the restaurants the tea leaves are all saved, and nothing about the cookshops goes to waste. Even the water in which potatoes and other vegetables are boiled is saved and sold for feeding hogs, and the bones are cut from the meat before it is sold in order that they may be used for the making of chopsticks. Old tins are saved and melted down for the solder.

There are public cookshops and soup houses kept by charity in some Chinese cities during the Winter, but as soon as Spring comes, these are shut up and the poor, as we say of the horses, are turned out to grass; for they have to live on the weeds and the greens. The necessities of the Chinese are, in fact, so few that a poor man can buy enough food to keep him alive for two cents a day and upon four dollars per month a man can support a family and put something away for his funeral.

A beggar

There is no land in the world where labour is so well organised as in China. The workman and the Government have been anxious to keep new inventions out of the country. The Chinese officials are afraid to introduce railroads rapidly for fear of the anger of the wheelbarrow pushers, cart drivers and boatmen. The opposition of these men was so great that until a few years ago, China had but one railroad, about 200 miles long. Of late, many other roads have been built and there are now several thousand miles opened, and other lines are projected which will enable one to reach all the Empire by train.

A Chinese hotel is a wonderful place. The surroundings would make one think of a barn yard. The rooms are stable-like sheds, about a court filled with donkeys which bray at all hours of the night, and with camels which cry like whipped babies. The bed is an oven-like brick ledge which fills one half of the room. It is heated by flues running under it. The fuel used is straw which quickly burns out, and the bed is stone cold before a new fire is lighted: one is therefore alternatively roasting and freezing. There are no springs and no bedding. One has to lie on a square of bass matting, and a heavy rug is used instead of blankets. So one rises from a Chinese bed with aching bones.

Nothing goes to waste

A Chinese store, as a rule, sells but one kind of goods, and stores of the same kind are usually to be found close together. There are streets lined with book stores and in some parts of the city we find scores of hat stores and fur stores and shoe stores. There are many things sold which would seem strange if offered for sale in this country. The drug stores, for instance, have sign boards advertising ground tiger's bones to strengthen faint hearts, and extracts of rat flesh to make the hair grow. There are shops which sell nothing but gold and silver paper which the Chinese burn at the graves of the dead, in order that they may not go without money into the land of spirits. There are large establishments which make and sell coffins, some of which cost hundreds of dollars. The Chinese often buy their coffins a long time before

Top: Gathering straws for fuel

Right: A pavement cobbler

death, and it is not unusual for a good son to present his father or mother with a fine coffin at New Year's. The father will keep the present in the best room of his house and will show it with pride to his neighbours.

There are many bird stores in Peking (see centre-spread). The Chinese are fond of pets and we shall see old men on the streets who carry little birds about with them on sticks which they hold in their hands. The legs of the bird are fastened to the stick by a string which permits it to fly a short distance. We find pigeons sold on the edge of the markets. These birds are the messengers of Peking, and they are perhaps the only pigeons in the world that whistle. As they fly through the air they make a noise which on the approach of a flock sounds like a whole school of boys blowing on tin whistles. This noise comes from

A weaver at work

whistles of wood which the people tie to the tails of their birds to scare off the hawks.

An old man

Government

The Emperor is an absolute monarch who rules his people through many officials. He has his Cabinet Ministers who have many officials and clerks under them and who advise him what he should do. Within

A country funeral

the last few years the Government has been changing. The Emperor has been making many reforms[52], and he has promised that the people shall have a constitution as soon as they have become educated enough to govern themselves. In a vast Empire like that of China, however, only a very few of the public matters can be submitted to the Emperor and the business of the Government was largely left to the officials, many of whom are very corrupt and take a large share of the public money for their own use.

A village in the countryside

There are eighteen provinces in China, each of which has a Governor with hundreds of officials under him. Each village has its own official or headman, which is usually selected from the best

[52] Bosworth points out that these reforms would have been carried out in the name of the boy Emperor P'u-Yi by the Prince Regent and other court officials. The court indeed attempted to speed up constitutional rule in the last years of Manchu rule, but they had only got as far as a draft constitution when the Republic took power in 1912.

educated by the villages concerned. The headman transacts all business connected with the village and its people. He details, daily, a night watch-man to guard the village from thieves &c during the night: this watchman beats a tom-tom during all hours of the night, thus signifying to neighbouring villages that all is quiet.

In China farm houses are not isolated like in Ireland. All farmers of a neighbourhood live close together, thus forming a village. This adoption is principally formed as a protection against thieves, of which China is invested. Not only is the headman responsible for the good conduct of his village, but every family is to a large extent responsible for the good conduct of the neighbourhood. If a boy commits a crime, his father, his elder brother and his teachers are sometimes punished as well as himself, for the Chinese say that if they had taught him properly, he would not have broken the laws. All cities have jails and the punishments connected with them are amongst the most cruel of the world, although many reforms are now being made. For small offences the criminal must wear about his neck a frame of heavy boards of about the size of the top of an ordinary kitchen table. It is made so that it can be opened and the man's neck fitted into a hole in the centre. This table arrangement weighs about 25 pounds, but some are so loaded with iron bars that they weigh as much as 90 pounds. Upon the top of the table on each side of the hole are posted strips of paper, describing the crime committed by the wearer, and the people stop and read them as the criminal passes through the streets. The worst crimes that can be committed are those by children against their parents. There is no other land where fathers and mothers have so much power. Parents have the right to whip their children to death if they will not obey. The punishment for striking a parent in China is death and now if one kills his father or mother he loses his head. Until recently the punishment for killing a parent was slicing to death: this

A farmer crushes his corn

A family of the interior

horrible punishment has now been abolished. Obedience to parents does not stop when children grow up, but it lasts until the death of the parents. Men and women are sometimes whipped by their fathers and mothers, and a man, after he is married, often asks his mother's permission if he wants to go out after dark.

Education

In passing through the streets of Peking, or those of any town in China, one cannot fail to see, even in the smallest and most unpretending shops, an ink slab, a stick of ink and the brushes used for writing, and probably someone engaged in noting down in a book what is evidently a series of business transactions. This produces the impression that the mass of the people are educated. A sign-board over a shop is proof that most of those who pass along can read it. Sign-boards would be of very little use to the illiterate; but in China it would be difficult, even in the smallest village, to find a shop that had not some character either painted or written to indicate its business (see centre-spread). This tendency to put up sign-boards, to have inscriptions on buildings, to place an engraved or written character on everything which they manufacture, struck me as very significant, and in this custom we might imitate them with benefit to ourselves.

All this is no new practice with the Chinese and the result is that the country is full of inscriptions. In the Confucian temple at Peking there are preserved ten 'Stone drums': these are said to date as far back as the celebrated Moabite stone[53], about 800 BC. The inscription is a very old character and relates a hunting expedition of an Emperor called Hsuan-wang. The stones were so highly valued that they were carried from one capital to another when the court migrated, and exact copies of them have been made so as to insure, in case of accident, the preservation at least of their character.

The whole surface, outside and inside, of the great bell of Peking is covered with characters. 'Curios' and goods of every description which are exhibited for sale have a character stamped on them to indicate the origin or manufacture. Biscuit manufacturers at home impress the names of their firms on what they sell: but the Chinaman is not behind them. In the meanest shop or stall hereabouts, buns may be seen with letters stamped on them in red colour. One day when walking through the street I met a man carrying home a duck he had just bought. It was killed, plucked and cooked and on its back was a large red stamp, which on enquiry turned out to be the name of the shop where it was bought. Whole rows of fowls may be seen for sale marked in this way. This will show that advertising is not unknown among the 'Celestials'.

[53] The Mesha Stele, a black basalt stone discovered in 1868, bearing an inscription by the 9th century BC Moabite King Mesha.

Large and attractive sign-boards are an attractive feature of Chinese shops and the words upon them are a strange mixture of the flowery literature of the land and the advertising instinct of a commercial people. I saw a list in Peking of sign-boards and a few samples of them will illustrate their general character. 'Shop of Heaven-sent Luck'. 'Tea-shop of Celestial Principles'. 'Mutton shop of Morning Twilight'. 'The Ten Virtues all complete'. There are also others such as 'The honest Pen-shop of Li' which implies that other pen-shops are not honest. 'The Steel shop of the pock-marked Wang' suggests that any peculiarity of a shopman may be used to impress the memory of customers. Snub noses, squint eyes, lame legs or hump backs might all be used in this way. A charcoal shop calls itself 'The Fountain of Beauty' and a place for the sale of coals indulges in the title of 'Heavenly Embroidery'. An oil and wine establishment is the 'Neighbourhood of Chief Beauty'. 'The Thrice Righteous' is a pretension one would scarcely expect from an opium shop.

The Chinese language is said to be composed of about 12,000 characters[54]. Of these only about 6,000 are in constant use. Our Bible, which is now printed in Chinese for use in these parts, is composed of 6,000 characters.

On entering the schools we shall find the children quite as bright as ourselves. They learn easily, they study hard and as a rule are anxious to have a good education. When a little boy starts to school for the first time, he carries a red visiting card with him and sometimes takes a present to the teacher. He is very polite and bows to the teacher when he enters or leaves the room. In the old style of schools he studies out loud and as we go through the streets of Peking we shall often hear a noise as though a dozen boys were fighting and howling. If we follow the noise we shall find that it comes from a school and that the boys are merely learning their lessons.

The system of teaching in China is very different from ours. They sit, either on their heels on the floor, or on benches before tables and they shout out at the top of their voices the words they are trying to commit, to get by heart the books which they are reading. If a boy stops shouting, the teacher thinks that he has stopped studying and gives him a caning. When they have learned a portion the pupils come to the schoolmaster, and, standing with their backs to him so that they cannot see the book in their master's hand, repeat what they have learned. It is a system of cramming in which the boy with the best memory stands highest and this seems to be the Chinese plan all through in education. I was rather astonished to find that, instead of homebooks, these little fellows were reading the Chinese classics. Imagine boys at home in a village school reading Plato, Homer or

---

[54]   Indeed there are more if all archaic, effectively dead, characters are included.

Chinese children and their toy cart

Milton and being able to repeat them from memory and you will realise the Chinese mode of education.

Education begins at a very early age in China: very small dumpy boys may be seen in the streets on their way to school with an armful of books in a satchel of blue cloth. In the interior, one day, I entered a school and the teacher was an old man with nearly twenty pupils. The boys do not sit on forms as in England, but there were a number of small tables, each with a boy or two sitting at them. The boys were very bright little fellows, some of whom knew a couple of words of English. When I entered the school all studying seemed to cease, for I found myself the centre of admiration. Even the old schoolmaster ceased work and directed his attention towards me. The boys who knew the few words of English circled around me, inspecting every part of my clothes. They tried to expound their knowledge of English as best they could, but it having no meaning whatsoever I could not understand it. Knowing a few words of their language, I tried a sentence or two to see if my knowledge of Chinese was any better than theirs of English. They got very much interested when they heard me speak a little of their tongue and brought over their books to me, every one being anxious that I should see his. Of course I did not know a character of the language, still I pretended to be much interested in the books and to satisfy all the boys I looked over each book in turn. They took to me so much that the schoolmaster lost all influence over them. They did not like the idea of me leaving so soon, but as I observed the old man in the corner getting restless and commencing to scold, I thought it better to leave and let him get on with his work.

The way the Chinese study arithmetic seems odd. In the new schools they study arithmetic similar to us, but they are also taught how to do sums quickly, by means of the Chinese counting box. This is a framework of wooden buttons strung upon wires. This counting box is used by all Chinese and with it they can make calculations quicker than we can with our paper and pencil.

All this is working up to the public examination system, which occupied so important a place in China that it may be called the core of the political and social fabric. As it is an old institution here, it would be well if it were carefully studied in reference to our own examination system, which is but a thing of yesterday. The principle on which it is founded is no doubt good, but still it is full of defects. A system which has been a thousand years at work, however perfect in its adaptation to the period when it began, is not likely to be in accordance with altered circumstances of the times now[55]. To be able to repeat the works of Confucius and Mencius is no doubt good, but cramming mere words into a child is not quite the best system of training. The

[55] The traditional Imperial Civil Service examination system had in fact been abolished in 1905, a few years before Hutchinson's observations.

mind has other and more important powers than that of mere memory. Limiting the source of knowledge to these old classic authors is another defect of the Chinese system. No sensible person would object to the study of ancient knowledge: but the limiting of a national system of education in any way must be a fault.

In China the educated class are said to be the haters of foreigners, the opponents of telegraphs, railways and of everything new. Their classic books date from the time of Confucius and with them the history of the world, or of intellectual thought, which is the essence of all history and knowledge, ceased at that time. The Chinaman has been grinding his teeth on these dry bones ever since, and he growls if any other dog should venture to approach. This education, confined to such narrow limits, has been going on till his mind is as compressed and diminutive as the small feet of the women of the country. The growth of a Chinese girl's feet is arrested in her infancy, and a literary man's mind has its growth arrested at the early date of Confucius. A woman here goes about much like a goat trying to walk on its hind legs, and an educated Chinaman seems equally incapable of treading the paths of modern knowledge; hence his total incapacity to comprehend the strange foreigners who have of late years invaded his soil. The whole civilisation of these foreigners began ages after the date of Confucius, and the educated Chinaman has not acquired in his training even the preliminary knowledge necessary to form a notion of their science and power.

Over the outside of the gateway of the Examination Hall at Peking there is this inscription: 'If you are high up in the classics, you will gain a scholarship'. And over the inside of the door 'Those who pass through this gate learn afterwards to govern the country'. This simply means that a knowledge of the classics is all that a man requires to entitle him to be a governor of men in the twentieth century in China.

The examination where the highest degree is obtained is held only once in three years, at Peking. The hall is divided into about 10,000 cells to accommodate the numbers who compete. There are similar examination halls in every provincial capital, where the first and second degrees are conferred; but the highest degree can only be obtained at Peking, at this triennial examination. It lasts nine days – that is, the 10,000 are shut up three times for three days and three nights for each 'go'. Tea and food are supplied. The students bring their own brushes – which are here used for pens – and ink. It is only when every man has taken his cell that the subject of examination is given out: and for three days and nights each is confined to a space about three feet square, where rest or sleep is almost impossible – where a stout man must have a difficulty getting in, or turning round when he is in. The cell is open, as there is no door in front, and a strict watch is kept that its occupant does not communicate with his neighbours on either side. It is a hard task, but the prize is great; and ambition, or vanity, seems as strong in the Chinaman's soul as it amongst ourselves. With them these literary degrees bring not only honour and respect: they are the step to position, wealth and rank. Even in the lower degrees, when the news reaches a village or town that one belonging to it has been successful, there are public rejoicings and the name of the successful candidate is placed over his father's door. To gain the prize at the Peking examination is a very high honour. They are entitled 'One of the Ten Thousand' – this very title telling how few can receive it, for it is only conferred once in three years. We are apt to associate competitive examinations with young men as the candidates; but such is not the case in China, and particularly at the Peking trial. The honour is so high, the temptation is so great, that men come up time after time till they are old and grey – men of seventy and eighty continuing to compete. It is not an uncommon occurrence to find at last their dead bodies in the cell. Ambition and hope have led them on till their physical powers were no longer sufficient for the ordeal and they succumb in the midst of it. Such is the end of some literary careers in China. In many cases where aspirants for honours have persevered, and without success, till they reach the advanced age of eighty, the Emperor confers some title upon them as a reward for such continued endeavours. In addition to the rank and position which these literary degrees command, there are Confucian temples where, if any should attain to popular fame and celebrity, he may hope for a tablet with an inscription which will transmit his name and reputation down to posterity.

The number of stone tablets for memorial and other objects erected all over the country is one of the many evidences of the literary education so earnestly coveted: and the respect paid to them is one of the good features in the character of the population. Old inscriptions are built into walls to preserve them; large stone tablets are standing in public thoroughfares and never seem to receive an injury. All written characters are respected by the Chinese. There are men employed who go about collecting all scraps of paper with writing upon them; these are carefully burned and I was told that the ashes are sent out to sea and thrown into it. There are societies formed principally of literary men in every part of China, who employ functionaries to do all this, and it is done from the idea that writing is so good and worthy, and is of such advantage to men, that it should not suffer any desecration and be always treated with respect. This reminds one of the Mahomedan's rule, not to burn any bit of paper, but it should have the name of 'Allah' upon it, the result being that with them also scraps of paper are very much respected.

There are very few girls schools. Until recently the Chinese have not thought that women needed much education and so very few girls go to school. What the proportion may be of educated Chinese women, it would be impossible to say. Foreign missionaries in large towns and ports have now taken this matter up and opened many girls' schools.

Pidgin English

In the Legations at Peking, Chinese is the language of communication between English men and the natives. This is because the language is studied there by those who must speak it in their official capacity. But in the open ports quite another language is spoken. It is now known as 'Pidgin English'[56]. This form of speech struck me very much and I have a theory to propose respecting it. It is not my purpose to trace words back through the dim ages which have gone but to suggest probabilities as to the future forms of speech among the 'Celestials'. The knowledge of the past of all language is as yet only in a very theoretical state; and in the nature of things, all speculation as to its future must be equally so. My theory rests on the assumption of the continued dominance of a race which will, by means of trade or conquest, retain a powerful influence in China. Still, no-one who knows China and is acquainted with the powers and influence of Westerners in the East will doubt that we shall not only maintain the position we have acquired but that most probably that position will become stronger; and our relations with the people become more intimate and powerful than ever.

A Chinese woman of the interior off to market

Taking all this for granted, we may consider what will be the future of that strange jargon known as 'Pidgin English', a language resulting from the meeting of East and West in the ports of China. This language, if such it may be called, derives its name from a series of changes in the word 'Business'. The early traders in China made constant use of this word, and the Chinaman contracted it to 'busin', and then through the change of 'pishin' it has assumed the form Pidgin. In this form it still retains its original meaning and people talk of whatever business they may have in hand as their 'Pidgin'. All mercantile transactions between the Chinese and the Europeans are carried on in this new form of speech. Domestic servants, male and female, have to learn it to qualify themselves for situations with the 'Outer Barbarians'; but the newest and most important feature of all is that the Chinese generally are, to a certain extent, adopting this language[57]. This is owing to the fact that men of different provinces

[56] There are of course, in the Caribbean and in Papua New Guinea for example, other forms of Pidgin English of which Hutchinson would not have been aware.

[57] Bosworth notes that Chinese in general were unlikely to be adopting pidgin. Some, he feels, may have used it with each other in the Treaty Ports. It is true that Chinese cannot understand some other dialects of their language: but they have the script in common. Bosworth supposes that 'the former Chinese language now only spoken in south China' is Hakka, which would not in any case have anything to do with the language of the Manchus. It is true that the non-Chinese invasions of China's north drove many Chinese to the south, and some southern dialects are much older than the Mandarin Chinese which is the official dialect of today's China.

cannot understand each other's dialect. The former Chinese language is now only spoken in South China. This language is composed of five different sounds and is a sort of mixed dialect with the Manchu. This, it is said, was brought about by the tribes from the north coming in, and taking possession of North China they drove the Chinese southwards.

It may be premature to call 'Pidgin English' a language. It is only the beginning of one. Although ideas can be expressed by it, it is in a most defective condition: so much so that when an Englishman, when he first reaches China, is very much amused at what seems to him a relic of Babel. If it should be his fate to remain in the country, he dislikes to adopt it. His sense of good manners makes it distasteful to him to speak such a jargon, for it sounds like making a fool of the party addressed: but here we get an evidence of the power of growth which this infantile speech is possessed of, for however reluctant anyone may be to speak it, he is forced by the necessity of the case to do so. I was traveller for only a few years in China, but I found myself obliged to acquire the habit of speaking what seemed to me, at first, nonsensical rubbish. I could not get on without it. One morning in Peking, I left my quarters very early and without any breakfast. After a couple of hours walk through the city, I secured such an appetite that I was tempted to visit the Y.M.C.A. for the purpose of having a breakfast: I called the 'boy' – servants in China are called 'boys', in fact this is one of the words of 'Pidgin English' – and expressed my wishes in the usual way of talk. The 'boy' went off smiling as if he understood my meaning: but as he did not come back I made enquiries to the manager. He asked what I said to the 'boy' and I repeated the words as nearly as I could recollect them, to the effect that I wanted some breakfast, and would like it immediately. I was then told that I might as well have talked Greek to him, and that I ought to have said 'Catchy some chow-chow chop-chop'. 'Chow-chow' is understood in this as something to eat, and the last double word is equivalent to 'quick quick'. Had I been a comic actor and the ordering of my breakfast been a farce, it might have been possible to feel that I should be saying the right thing in this way. That not being my 'Pidgin' I felt reluctant to do it; but when eating, drinking and all your wants are found to depend upon its use, you soon give in; and here is the source of growth in the language, and the reason why it advances and spreads in China.

One would suppose that such a mode of speaking could only have a temporary existence, but these facts are given to show that such will not be the case, and that there is no chance of its dying out.

On the contrary, we have the Chinese now adopting it among themselves as a means of communication. There is nothing new in this: it is only history repeating itself. We have on record the growth of other languages which must have begun under similar conditions. A notable example of this is the language known as Hindustani. Its origin dates from the Mahomedan conquest of India. It was named the 'Dordoo'[58] or 'Camp language', because it grew up in the camp of the invaders. The conquerors and the conquered spoke entirely different languages and as a consequence their means of communication at first must have been only fragmentary. Each, however, acquired broken bits of the other's speech, and time at last welded the whole into a language. It has now a grammar based on the Hindu or Sanskrit, and an ample dictionary in which it will be found that about three-fourths of the words belong to the language of the invading power. This has long been the language of India. Many languages are spoken there, but this one will carry you over nearly the whole length and breadth of the country. The pure Farsee, or Persian, remained and is still considered the *burra-bat* or high court language. Of course the camp might jabber any combination of sounds it found most suited to its wants, but the dignity of a court could not submit to the introduction of such barbarisms.

For the same reason 'Pidgin English' would scarcely be a fit language for St. James's or Windsor Castle. Imagine a Chinese Embassy with the principal personage in it explaining to His Majesty that he is 'one piecey ambassador, that belongey my pidgin', 'Emperor of China one very muchy big piecey Emperor', etc. Clearly this style of talk is not likely to be used for diplomatic purposes for some time. 'Pidgin English' is as yet in so rudimentary a state that to talk of its grammar would only raise a smile among those who are familiar with it. When you hear it spoken it sounds like an utter defiance of all grammar; and yet if we are to remain in the country as the Mahomedans did in India, and go on extending our commerce, a common language is an absolute condition of the case, and this new form of speech must make way.

Already its idiomatic forms are becoming understood. Chinese modes of expression are curiously mixed with English ones. The interrogative form is purely Chinese. Suppose you wish to ask a man if he can do anything for you, the sentence is put 'Can do? No can do?' and the reply is given by repeating whichever sentence expresses his abilities. It is the same with 'Understand? No understand?' 'Piecey' is a word that is largely used and clearly has its origin in our own language of commerce which talks of a 'piece of goods'; but with the Chinaman everything is a 'piecey'. He does not say 'one man' but 'one piecey man'. There are a few Hindustani words in use, such as 'chit' for a letter, 'tiffin' for lunch and 'bund' for a quay or embankment. The word 'Mandarin' is from the Portuguese; 'dios' from the same language became 'joss' and is a well-known word in China – Joss-House or God-House, meaning a temple,

[58] Urdu

being derived from it. 'Savvy' is from the Portuguese and is always used as the equivalent of 'know'. To have, or to be connected with, is always expressed by 'belongey'. If you wish to say that an article is not yours, you express it thus: 'That no belongey me'. This terminal -ey of 'belongey' is one of the forms which is peculiar to this new language. From it we have 'supposey', 'talkey', 'walkey', 'catchey' etc. The Portuguese 'savvy', which is one of the first words in use, may be the original root of this form. Many of the words in use are of unknown origin. In a number of cases the English suppose them to be Chinese, while the Chinese, on the other hand, take them to be English. 'Chow-chow' is one of these words. I heard a Chinese 'Boy' on one occasion tell another of his country-men that 'Chow-chow' was the English for 'food': up to that time I always thought it was the Chinese for 'food'. A good many Chinese words are of course used, but the bulk of the vocabulary is English.

It is not very satisfactory to look forward even to the bare possibilities of such a caricature of our tongue becoming an established language. Should this ever be the result, translations into it of our classic authors will become a necessity. It is fearful even to think of translations of Shakespeare and Milton turned into Pidgin English.

6 *The great sights of China*

SINCE the Peking to Kalgan railway was completed a few years ago, the trip to the Nan-K'ou Pass and Great Wall has been greatly facilitated. Formerly this trip was an affair of four or five days, and the necessary provisions had to be taken for the journey. I have travelled over some bad roads in China but none to compete in this respect with the one from Peking to Nan-K'ou. There are said to be a few good roads in China. In my travels I have never met with any of them, and certainly the one to Nan-K'ou is not one of them. I have some little idea of what a trip to Nan-K'ou by road is like, from my experience in reaching the Summer Palace, which lies only about ten miles out from Peking, in that direction.

During my stay in Peking, I got a small party together for the purpose of visiting Nan-K'ou and the Great Wall. Before undertaking such a trip, we thought it advisable to make inquiries as to the best and most interesting way of doing the journey. The railway, of course, would be the quickest way, but as we were out on a sort of sightseeing expedition, we did not like the idea of going by rail as that would mean having to cut the Summer Palace and Ming tombs out of our programme. We asked a few residents, who had previous experiences of all these places, and they advised us to first take a ride out to the Summer Palace on ponies, return again to Peking, and make the journey to Nan-K'ou by rail, taking in the Ming tombs on donkeys from Nan-K'ou.

The Imperial Summer Palace

This we all agreed to and the next morning saw us off on horseback to the Summer Palace. There were four of us in the party – all on ponies. The road was fairly good for a couple of miles out of the city, after which it became a cart-track and got worse as we continued. Certainly it had the appearance of once being a good road, and we were told that it was the great Imperial road to the Ming tombs. That would be during the Ming dynasty, which ended in 1644, so that for more than two and a half centuries this road has not been used for its original purpose, and the present dynasty have no interest in it, for all their tombs are somewhere in Manchuria. That section to the Summer Palace has been used as an Imperial way in recent years, but that does not seem to have benefited it in the way of repairs. There is a Board of Works in Peking, but whether roads and ways come within its province or not I cannot say. I am told that a mandarin may regularly draw the necessary funds for keeping this particular road in repair, and perhaps remits part of the cash to someone, who pays a fraction of it to another person, who employs somebody else to write reports on its condition, which are no doubt sent in to Peking to the Board of Works, declaring that all is perfection.

There are old and very fine bridges on this road more or less in ruins. These bridges are constructed of very large and well-hewn stones, but they stand unconnected with the road on each side, as if a deluge had swept past and carried the banks away. It is only by a struggle up a steep bank of earth and over some of the fallen blocks of stone that the bridge can be reached by carts and animals. The road had got so deep in some places that we could only get a glimpse occasionally of the fields as we drove along. The road leads for a considerable distance through a valley. A connected system of lakes formed the central part of this valley. Here and there the lake was only of mud, and at times the lake and mud filled up the whole breadth of the road, so that there was no avoiding it, and carts had a number of animals to pull them through. The mud dries in summer and is blown away in dust by the wind. This after many years is the cause of the road becoming a deep ravine.

The towns along this line are in as remarkable a condition as the roads. They have high walls, with bastions like the walls of Peking. These high walls are tumbling: huge masses of the brickwork may be seen which have slidden down, leaving a practicable breach should an enemy ever appear; but enemies are not likely to give trouble: even friends avoid them. There is a system which is known here by the word 'squeezing' and is said to be largely practised by those in power. To avoid being treated like lemons, people prefer to live outside the gates, and the result is a thriving suburb, which flourishes on what is now considered the safest side of the walls. If one should enter by the high portal of one of these pretentious fortifications, expecting to find busy streets and an active population, he will be slightly disappointed. The interior is more like a wilderness than anything else. There may be a house here and there among the wretched thoroughfares which pass for streets; but pariah dogs and pigs seem to be left in possession – perhaps they remain because they are not liable to the squeezing process. The roads, bridges and great walls of these towns all tell of a time when there was a government in the country which did something; their present condition tells of a government which is defunct, and only waits its time to be removed.

After a ride of about two hours over this bad road, the Imperial Summer Palace was sighted in the distance. A very noticeable feature about the Summer Palace grounds and which makes it visible for a considerable distance is the high hill in the centre, covered with shrines. The Wan-Shou-Shan, which means the mountain of eternity or the mountain of 10,000 ages, is the beautiful spot on which the Imperial Palace was erected during the earlier parts of the present dynasty: its name in reality is Yi-Ho-Yuan. However it is like other places in China which have official names, and the one which the people generally use is Wan-Shou-Shan. Therefore the name, it seems, is derived from this picturesque mountain in the centre and does not refer to the palace grounds.

The only days on which foreigners are allowed to visit this palace are 5th, 15th and 25th of every Chinese month, when the Court is absent. Along the main road before the Main Porch of the Palace is reached are several *yamens* where the Court officials reside, and just before the main entrance there is a new building called the Wai-Wu-Pu[59] which is used as an entertainment and reception room for foreigners. In the immediate neighbourhood are many summer residences of princes and high dignitaries of state.

On entering the palace one is impressed by the fine buildings and scenery in which art and nature is combined. The principal feature of the Wan-Shou-Shan is a Buddhist temple all in porcelain, and very beautiful it is. I believe that 'majolica' would be a more correct word to use in describing this building[60]. It is formed of glazed earthenware, red, green and yellow predominating. It is one mass of ornament and Buddhist figures, and is the most beautiful specimen of that style of work that I saw in China. Many of the shrines round it have been destroyed, but this building is untouched.

The allied powers in the Taiping rebellion of 1860, I believe, entered this palace and ransacked it[61]. The same thing occurred again in 1900 when the Japanese and Russians took vengeance by ransacking and burning many places: they seemed to take delight in shivering mirrors with their bayonets and knocking the heads off the small yellow porcelain Buddhas outside the Myriad Buddha Temple (see centre-spread). Some of these things are still left in their ruinous state, but every effort is being made to restore it to perfect beauty. The building however escaped on both occasions: its protection in 1860 I believe is due to Lord Elgin[62], who gave orders that it was not to be interfered with.

The 'White Clouds' Temple, situated in the Summer Palace grounds, is one of the finest Buddhist temples in the neighbourhood of Peking,

[59] Literally meaning 'outside affairs department'.
[60] This would be the Temple of the Sea of Wisdom (Chi-Hui-Hai).
[61] Bosworth observes 'In 1860 an Anglo-French force did indeed ransack the Summer Palace. However, this was during an armed conflict that was unrelated to the Taiping rebellion (which was indeed ongoing at that time but further south). As retribution for the murder of allied negotiators, Lord Elgin gave the order for the Summer Palace to be burned to the ground. In the 1880s part of the complex was rebuilt. The nearby western-style palace buildings designed by the Jesuits were not rebuilt and have lain in ruins up till the present.'
[62] James Bruce, 8th Earl of Elgin and 12th Earl of Kincardine 1811–1863, son of the 7th Earl of 'Elgin Marbles' fame. He became High Commissioner to China in 1857.

The White Clouds Temple (Yun-Hui-Ssu)

The stone pagoda

built in the Indian style of architecture. This temple was originally begun under the Mongol Dynasty (1264–1368) but later was embellished under the Ming and present dynasties. It is a small bronze temple, and it was strange and instructive to see the original wooden forms of Chinese architecture here all repeated in metal. The interior of this temple was quite as interesting as the exterior, and a great change from those visited a few days before in Peking. This temple possessed a fine gallery of the Five Hundred Lohans or Disciples of Buddha.

In the centre of the palace grounds is a beautiful lake called Kun-Ming-Hu covering several square miles. Here and there are dotted small islands, promenades along the water's edge, pagodas as well as the residential quarters of the Imperial Court; also great ceremonial and audience halls for the reception of ministers and high officials. Along its water's edge with the marble railing are many ideal resting places, with enchanting panoramic scenes before them. There is a covered walk about a mile long, and through the inner court yards of the temple grounds are many pleasant promenades. The marble bridges are a very striking feature and show some marvellous feats of Chinese architecture (see centre-spread).

On the hill with its architectural buildings and terraces one can look over the island and Peking, and also see the mountains. The Tu-Teng or Precious Mountain pagoda makes a picturesque background and a pleasing feature is that of taking a boat ride on the lake and visiting the huge marble boat which when one gets on board, seems to mesmerise with the magnificent architecture. The same thing occurs when getting a view of the marble bridge which is just in rear of the boat. One feels it a great privilege to get a view of these interesting structures. The marble boat house is magnificent (see centre-spread). The whole is formed of hewn marble, morticed together. There is now a restaurant aboard it, where refreshments in European style can be obtained. This palace has been one of the most magnificent pleasure grounds that the world has ever seen. Since 1900 nothing has been spared to further beautify this dream-like Wan-Shou-Shan Palace.

In the background of the Summer Palace is a high stone pagoda, which stands as a reminder of former greatness. This pagoda stands on a hill about 200 feet high. Here rises the spring which supplies the lake in the centre of the Summer Palace. In the neighbourhood of this pagoda are also the walls of the old hunting park called Hsiang-Shan. We had lunch on return to the Summer Palace, after which we rode back again to Peking.

THE GREAT SIGHTS OF CHINA 113

The Peking to Kalgan Railway and the Great Wall of China

No time was lost on our return, for preparations had to be made for our trip to Nan-K'ou the following morning. It was decided to make a two days affair of this trip, therefore ample provisions had to be taken, which in this case was composed of a good supply of bread, preserved meat, tea, sugar and milk. Each one carried a cup, plate, knife and fork, there being a hotel somewhere near Nan-K'ou station where we could get water boiled and any small luxuries which one might feel inclined for: nothing was carried except the mere requirements for the trip.

Next morning saw us off again by the first train. From Legation Quarter it takes an hour's rickshaw ride to the Hsi-Chi-Men. Just outside this gate is the Hsi-Chen-Men station of the Peking – Kalgan Railway. The timetables of this railway are advertised in the papers and hotels. From the Hsi-Chen-Men the railway runs north to Nan-K'ou. The length from Peking to its terminus at Kalgan[63] is about 125 miles: the whole line is now open to traffic and most of the tourists go up to the top of the pass by travelling to Ch'ing-Lung-Ch'iao where the gates of the great inner wall of China are situated. Our journey to Nan-K'ou was about 100 miles: and on that long stretch there are only two stations, the other stopping places being merely sidings to allow trains to pass, this being only a single line. The first station reached was Ch'ing-Ho, in whose neighbourhood is the Summer Palace, Wan-Shou-Shan. The other is Sha-Ho from where a road leads to the Ming Tombs.

The railway to Kalgan and above it part of the Great Wall

We had expected to witness a very exciting ride to Nan-K'ou but were disappointed, for the railway is practically level for that distance. The Peking to Kalgan railway has been one of the most wondrous feats ever accomplished by an engineer, and should figure highly amongst other engineering feats of the world. Up to Nan-K'ou there is nothing marvellous about the construction. Between Nan-K'ou and Kalgan are two ranges of mountains with a picturesque valley in the centre. This railway runs through these mountains (see centre-spread) and over the valley, so one can imagine what obstacles engineers had to surmount in its construction. From Nan-k'ou to Pa-Ta-Ling is a distance of 10 miles. On arrival at Nan-K'ou we decided to continue our journey to the height of the mountainous pass at Pa-Ta-Ling in order to witness this wonderful piece of engineering.

From Nan-K'ou two engines are employed, one in front and one in rear, for the railway in this short distance of 10 miles rises to an

[63] Kalgan is today known as Zhangjiakou.

altitude of nearly 2,000 feet. One wonders when passing along the route about the filling-in of great embankments, which in places reach over 60 feet in height. The most striking features are the high bridges standing on concrete pillars, so as to give safety in crossing over the violent mountain streams which during the rainy season flood large portions of the pass.

Along the road the traveller passes first the great Customs barrier of Chu-Yung-Kuan with an interesting stone gate which is beautifully carved. At this point the railway traverses the first of three tunnels on this section of the line. The first tunnel reached is about 1,200 feet long. A second Customs barrier is at Wu-Kwei-T'ou, meaning the Five Rich Heads. The train on clearing this tunnel travels for a short distance and enters another of 456 feet long which is at the point called Shi-Fei-Ssu. The third and largest tunnel is at the height of the pass at Pa-Ta-Ling where also the Great Wall is crossed. This tunnel is about two and a half miles in length. It was cut through from several sections: from the Kalgan extremity and from the Pa-Ta-Ling point, as well as from the centre. For this latter cutting a 200 feet shaft was sunk, just from the top of the mountain where the gate of the Great Wall stands. It will be interesting to know that this shaft was sunk and the whole tunnel worked entirely by Chinese engineers and labour. The Chinese engineer staff, we were told, were all American and English graduates. The railway engineering along this line is very well carried out; and great precautions are taken to avert any accident. There are, at distances of about a mile, sidings for use in case of emergency. This railway is now completed up to its present terminus, Kalgan, on the borders of Mongolia. From Kalgan it is proposed to continue the railway through Mongolia and through the desert of Gobi, in order to reach Urga and Kiakhta on the Russo-Siberian frontier, where it will connect up with the Trans-Siberian Railway at Irkutsk. This then will be the shortest route to Europe.

Pa-Ta-ling is the highest point of the Nan-K'ou Pass. Here the inner section of the Great Wall of China runs. The Great Wall is indeed the most wonderful structure in the world and quite worthy of its place amongst the world's seven great wonders. It was originated by Shi-Huang-Ti, the first universal monarch of all China, reigning in 221 BC It commences at the seaside resort of Shan-Hai-Kwan[64] where the greatest proportion of the foreign residents of Peking and Tientsin generally reside during the summer months, also the troops have their camping areas quite close to the sea shore. It runs over the mountains clear across the northern boundary of China proper, just south of the vast tributary provinces of Manchuria and Mongolia until it reaches the desert of Gobi, north of Tibet. It was built as a protection against

[64] Foreigners actually had their resort homes built at nearby Pei-Tai-Ho (today Beidaihe and still a popular resort).

A stretch of the Great Wall

the Mongolian hordes who often invaded North China. The whole length of the wall is about 2,000 English miles – the Chinese call it the Wan-Li-Ch'ang Ch'eng, or 'Myriad Mile Wall'. It is a structure 22–30 feet in height and 20–25 feet in thickness. At intervals of about 100 yards there are towers of some forty feet in height. It is composed of bricks each weighing over 21 pounds: they are each about 15 inches long, 7 inches wide and 3 inches thick.

It was built right over the tops of the mountains, and in one place it goes over a peak which is more than 5,000 feet high. It climbs the steepest of crags which never could require defence. In some parts there is no clay within 30 miles of it. The bricks were all made by hand and many of the hills which the wall crosses are so steep that it is said that the Chinese had to tie bricks to the backs of sheep and goats in order to get them to the builders. At the time that this wall was built, there were few cattle and horses in China, and every foot of it was made without the aid of machinery. The Chinese historians say that it took an army of 300,000 men to protect the builders, and millions of people must have been employed upon it. They state that this vast work was begun and completed in the short space of ten years.

I feel quite proud of having the opportunity of seeing parts of these wonderful constructions, especially the Great Wall, which is in one way like the Suez Canal. Looking on one side you see one country and on the other side another country. One cannot help marvelling at the condition of such an aged structure, built thousands of years ago, and only in some parts can be seen traces of ruin. One of the places where it is broken away is at Shan-Hai-Kwan and we were able to run up one side in China and down the other side into Mongolia.

Just below Pa-Ta-Ling there is a fort with a good-sized village. Its name is Chu-Yung-Kuan. There is a portion of the inner wall here which is said to be very old. The place is celebrated as being the spot at which Genghis Khan was successfully stopped in his efforts to force the pass[65]. There stands a very ancient arch here, full of sculptures and inscriptions. As this erection stands by itself and has no relation to the walls of the fort, it presents the appearance of a triumphal arch. The sculptures are chiefly on the inside and consist of figures of Buddha. The date of the arch is 1345. The inscription is repeated in six different characters, some of which are almost unknown.

The most striking feature of the Nan-K'ou pass and one which a traveller cannot fail to see, is the enormous amount of traffic that passes through it. This is a most interesting and historic point, for through this pass between Nan-K'ou and Kalgan, China transports her products through Mongolia towards Siberia as well as to other parts of Europe, and had transported them thus long before Vasco da Gama discovered the sea route to India and China. This famous route was also known to the Venetian traveller Marco Polo who came overland from Europe to China in AD 1274. Leaving history aside, it is interesting even nowadays to observe how through this narrow pass caravan after caravan climbs up and down bringing products from Mongolia to China and vice versa – tea and other Chinese and foreign products such as kerosene etc into Mongolia.

From appearances it seemed as if a good road had once existed, but like other roads through China it has been terribly neglected. The Nan-K'ou pass is renowned for being stony. Most mountain passes left in a natural state are stony, but this one is pre-eminently so. The road being in ruins now helps to increase the quantity of stones for which the pass is renowned. When in good order, it must have been much used, for there are deep ruts in the stones caused by the traffic of cart wheels, which must have taken many a year to produce. At the present day carts cannot pass. We saw portions of them, such as the wheel etc, being taken through on the backs of mules. As this is the route of all caravans going to Siberia and Russia, besides being one of the

---

[65] Hutchinson may have set down here what he heard, rather than what accords with the facts. The 'arch' described in the same paragraph was actually built during the Mongol dynasty and had nothing to do with the 'halting of Genghis Khan'. It is true that under Genghis Khan the Mongols seized the Beijing area around 1215 from another non-Chinese tribal kingdom; perhaps there was a battle there at that time. In *China's Historical Sites*, published by the China Foreign Publishing Co. (HK) Ltd., Hong Kong, 1987, there is the following description: 'The Cloud Platform of the Juyongguan (Chü-Yong-Kuan) Pass is situated within the pass in Changping County of Beijing. The Platform is the foundation across a road for a pagoda, which was destroyed long ago. It was constructed . . . in the late Yuan (Mongol) Dynasty (1339). The 9.5 metre high platform is built completely of white marble. At the center of the platform there is an arch through which carriages and horses can pass. Inside the cave arch are sculptures. . . On two walls are sculptures of the four heavenly kings with inscriptions of Buddhist scriptures and a description of construction of the Pagoda in six styles of ancient written characters.'

principal lines into Mongolia, the traffic is immense. Mules, donkeys and camels are constantly going and coming in large and small groups.

We saw hemp paper, oil, felt, grapes &c coming in, together with sheep, goats and bullocks, for the Peking market. Soda from Kalgan is an article of trade that comes by this pass from China.

Heavy carts either loaded with goods or with travellers attract attention. Especially when they are going the downward way they have an extra horse in the rear which holds the cart back so as not to lose its equilibrium. Otherwise it would fall over the precipice into the river below. So therefore for pleasure it cannot be recommended to travel by these springless Chinese carts, for one never knows what may happen to the near horse, should it stumble and fall, the consequence may be the end of sight-seeing for the tourist. The best conveyance is that of horse-back which takes about four hours to travel from Nan-K'ou to the height of the pass. Along the most southern part of the pass the gradient is 1:30 feet; the section from Ch'ing-Lung-Ch'iao towards Kalgan has only a grade of 1:70 feet.

The mule litter is a very striking vehicle and the only one that can nowadays traverse the Nan-K'ou pass. This curious looking construction of conveyance is used principally for carrying passengers, but the Chinese make it a vehicle for all purposes. It is a very clever invention and no doubt was introduced to cope with the bad roads of China. It is a sort of kennel box covered with blue canvas and swung between two poles, each about thirty feet long. These poles stick out in front and behind, forming two pairs of shafts in which the mules walk or trot along in single file. The litter is open in front, and if used for passengers, it is furnished with blankets where one has to crawl in and lie down, being jolted by the mules as they carry you over the roads.

When I first visited Peking, I was struck with the amount of camels which occasionally passed through the streets. I was told that these beasts formed the principal transport to and from Mongolia. Here at Nan-K'ou I witnessed trains of forty to sixty camels one after another moving to and fro through the pass, all laden with various kinds of products. Some trains were over a mile long and it was very striking to see them winding along the route, in the distance. Six of these beasts are tied one to another by ropes fastened to sticks thrust through the flesh of their noses. The last camel of each six has about his neck an iron bell as big around as a stove-pipe and about a foot long. They move in single file with soft velvety steps, silently and contemptuously along. This keeps up a ding-dong as long as he moves and announces to the Mongolian driver that his six of the caravan are all right.

Camels refresh themselves

Camels in Peking

The Ming Tombs

The return trip from the height of the pass (actually 2,060 feet), if one hires a donkey, takes about three hours. From Pa-Ta-Ling we returned again to Nan-K'ou and, as recommended, put up in the Nan-K'ou railway hotel for the night: it was erected at the time the railway opened for traffic. This is a European hotel and has fairly good accommodation for travellers. The rate charged including board is $6.00 for staying overnight and they provide donkeys or chairs for excursions for which they charge $2.00 a day, including the coolie. Having a good supply of provisions along with us, we did not trouble the proprietor very much in that line. He looked after us very well: we had water boiled whenever required and all little knick-knacks to complete our dish were easily obtained. Next morning we were on our way to the Ming tombs, having hired donkeys for this trip. They are on the southern side of the range of hills upon which the Great Wall is constructed. We were now on an extension of the same road which leads to the Summer Palace from Peking. This section of the road is in the usual state of dilapidation and forms a strong contrast to the fine marble arches erected at intervals across it. These marble arches had struck me as being more like what one would expect to find about a palace than on a country road. This had already explained itself: for in former years this had been an Imperial Road from Peking to the tombs.

On nearing the tombs, a number of partly destroyed marble bridges and other works of art are passed and then we came to a fine entrance gateway of marble and an enormous *P'ai-Lou* of very fine carved marble which stands about fifty feet high and eighty feet wide and has five openings. Just beyond this *P'ai-Lou* is a tower like building in which stands a huge stone monument on a large and beautifully carved tortoise. The inscription on the monument, which gives praise by the most famous Manchu Emperor to the Ming Dynasty, states that in the fiftieth year of the reign of Emperor Ch'ien-Lung (AD 1786) this stone was erected. Four stone pillars decorated with carvings stand on each corner of the towers.

On passing through we reached what is considered the principal sight of the place, which is about three miles from the Yung-Lê temple. This is a long approach bordered on each side with sculptured animals, all fully the size of life. There are in all about twenty animals and twelve human figures. Among the animals are lions, camels, elephants, horses, mules and mythical figures. The human figures are of warriors, mandarins and priests. This stone population of man and beast extends for at least a good half mile and ends by another triple gate. Each of these statues is cut from a single block of marble. The monster elephants are 13 feet high, 14 feet long and seven feet wide. The human figures are each about 9 feet high. When you reach the end of this sculptured avenue, you are in the centre of an amphitheatre of hills. One can see in the distance what seem to be country houses surrounded by trees all round the base of the hills. These are the tombs called 'Shih-San-Ling' or Thirteen Tombs, this being their number. It would have been impossible to visit the whole of them, and as they are all of the same type we made for the principal one, a slight description of which will do for them all. Their arrangement is very important as bearing on the old ideas of tomb construction, and particularly that of the barrow or tumulus graves. In these tombs, which are formed in a semi-circle, are buried the bodies of the Emperors of the Ming Dynasty. In the centre stands the great temple dedicated to the Emperor Yung-Lê and in rear of the temple is a mound erected to this same Emperor. It was this ruler of the great Ming Dynasty (1368–1644) who transferred his court from Nanking to Peking in AD 1421. This temple is a favourite spot for picnic parties and while visitors are sitting about in groups attending to the wants of the inner man, they can also feast their eyes on some magnificent scenery, and numerous thoughts fly through one's mind as one gazes at the huge stone figures.

The graves all over China are simply small mounds of earth and the Imperial tombs of the Mings are also mounds, but much larger. We visited the tomb of Yung-Lê, the third of the race, who died in 1424. A large mound about 600 or 700 feet in diameter forms the sepulchral part of this monument. It is surrounded by a high wall of brick and planted with trees. There are many important buildings in front of this mound, the principal of which is the great ancestral hall of Yung-Lê.

The marble animals which mark the approach to the Ming Tombs

One of the magnificent marble elephants at
the Ming Tombs

In the central point of this hall, in a shrine, is placed the ancestral tablet of the Emperor. From the position of the altars it is easily understood that the principal form of ceremony which takes place here is tomb worship – or the worship of deceased ancestors. In the rear of the temple is a great forest where one can see trees of enormously great age and huge in circumference.

We had lunch in the great ancestral hall of Yung-Lê. The Chinese do not associate any ideas of desecration with the use of a temple as a house. They use them in this way themselves, and offer them for the accommodation of travellers, so that we were committing no impropriety in taking our lunch in front of the altar of this deceased ancestor. After lunch we returned again to Nan-K'ou and reached Peking by the evening train.

7 *Eventful times*

Summer Camp

OUR summer camp was situated about two miles from the town of Shan-Hai-Kuan and beside the sea, the port of Ch'in-Huang-Dao being only a short distance away. The Great Wall of China, built 200 years BC and 1400 miles long, runs from the Desert of Gobi to the sea at Shan-Hai-Kuan, quite close to our camp.

The Great Wall climbs away from the sea near Shan-Hai-Kuan

Our quarters here were wooden huts, most of which leaked badly in wet weather. There was a splendid rifle range and the country around, though mountainous, was ideal for field training. Six Companies went to camp each summer while two remained on detachment at Tientsin and Peking respectively. A large river flowed into the sea near our camp. As this river was much cleaner than the Yellow Sea, it was made use of for Bathing, Aquatic Sports &c. Private Shanks took pneumonia at Shan-Hai-Kuan, which proved fatal.

On the occasion of the Coronation of H.M. King George V in 1910, the Battalion honoured the occasion by firing the Feu de Joie from the Great Wall of China. For a British Regiment to honour such an occasion from the Great Wall of the 'Celestial' Empire of China must be unique in the annals of British history.

Three comrades lost in north China: Private Samuel Shanks on the left

The gun-carriage at one of the funerals

To reach Shan-Hai-Kuan from Tientsin two routes are available. We usually travelled to camp by rail, on the Imperial Railway to Shan-Hai-Kuan station, a distance of 180 miles. Returning to Tientsin however, we entrained at Shan-Hai-Kuan for Ch'in-Huang-Dao, thence by coastal steamer up the winding Pei-Ho River. Though it took us longer this way, it was the most interesting route.

In 1910 Lieutenant-Colonel A. J. Hancocks assumed command in succession to Lt. Col. C. J. L. Davidson who retired, Capt Pike relieving Capt. Smythe as Adjutant.

We always looked forward to camp, if only to get away from the summer heat and mosquitoes, both very unpleasant in the closed up Barracks at Tientsin. In addition to the annual musketry course, we enjoyed the shooting competitions and above all field exercises with ball ammunition. Good shooting was encouraged, the Company with the highest average score usually heading the Battalion on route marches. Keen competition existed for Battalion and Company Shot and Marksmen's badges. I remember, in 1910, Colour Sergeant Maguire was Battalion Shot, I having run him very close in that year.

The graves of two of the comrades

Relaxing at camp: walking the greasy pole

Revolution

In 1908 the Empress Dowager of China died. She was a wicked ruler who controlled a most corrupt government at Peking. At this time the Chinese were very discontented with these Manchu rulers. The young prince who succeeded her had practically no control over the Government. A revolution was bound to come. Sun-Yat-Sen who was educated in England[66], saw his chance. He mobilised a force in the

---

[66] In fact he received the bulk of his education in Hawaii and Hong Kong. He did spend some time in London as an adult and did further reading there.

The Officers of the Royal Inniskilling
Fusiliers, Tientsin, 1912
From the album of Lt. Col. M. F. Hammond-Smith MC,
at the Regimental Museum of the Royal Inniskilling
Fusiliers, Enniskillen

Front row, left to right: Capt. J. N. Crawford,
Capt. G. W. Kenny, Maj. E. W. Blennerhassett,
Lt. Col. A. J. Hancocks, Capt. & Adj. W. Pike,
Maj. F. G. Jones

Second row: Capt. G. W. Robinson, 2nd. Lt.
R. B. Shubrick, Lt. J. J. Kirkpatrick

Third row: 2nd. Lt. E. W. H. Raymond, Capt.
G. W. Willock, Lt. H. W. Dickinson, 2nd. Lt.
G. R. O'Sullivan

Fourth row: Lt. Q. M. W. A. Morris, Lt. J. R. C.
Dent, Lt. H. L. Crofton

Southern Provinces away from Peking, early in 1911[67]. To his satisfaction this force, as he marched north, was like a snowball: the further he travelled, the larger it became. By the time the Government got aware of this force, it had grown so large that in the end the Government Forces, most of whom had joined the rebels, were overthrown the following year.

[67] Bosworth writes: 'Sun-Yat-Sen was actually not in China when the Wuchang/Han-K'ou uprising by disaffected army units occurred on October 10, 1911: (he was travelling in the American mid-west, drumming up support for a republic in China). Rather than a rebel 'force' marching north, other uprisings occurred in scattered parts of the country, leading provinces to break from the empire one by one. An opportunistic military officer, Yuan Shikai, was named premier of the Imperial government in Peking and staged a successful counter-offensive in some areas. At the same time, he opened negotiations with the rebel groups, led by Sun's umbrella organization. Sun-Yat-Sen did not return to China until December. He became provisional President of the new republic on January 1, 1912. A month later, however, he stepped down in favour of Yuan Shikai who had helped negotiate the abdication of the Emperor and the effective end of resistance by imperial troops'.

We left Shan-Hai-Kuan for the last time on 20th August 1911, arriving at Tientsin the following day. By this time it had become known that we were to sail for Deolali, India early in October.

Sabotage by Imperial troops at the great railway bridge[68] (see also page 27)

The Revolution by this time was in full swing and as usual rumours were flying around that, should it reach Tientsin, we might have to stay in case the foreign Concessions needed our protection. No further orders came through. The *H. T. Somali* arrived at Ch'in-Huang-Dao early in October with the Somerset Light Infantry who were to relieve us.

Revolutionary artillery on the battlefield at Han-K'ou

The British at Tientsin and Peking were becoming alarmed. Our Ambassador by this time was finding it difficult to get information through to England. All sorts of rumours were going around. We entrained at Tientsin, according to schedule on 24th October 1911. The many friends seeing us off had misgivings as to whether the move, even now, would not be cancelled. We duly arrived at Ch'in-Huang-Dao, where the *H. T. Somali* lay at anchor. We embarked and after two

---

[68] This and the following three photographs were not taken by Hutchinson, although he used them in his lantern slide lectures and included them in his album. He did not leave an indication of their source.

Marines guard the Concessions in Han-K'ou

days on board, an advance party under the charge of Lt. and Quartermaster W. A. Morris with a fatigue party disembarked and returned again to Tientsin to make the necessary arrangements for our return. The Battalion disembarked the following day, leaving on board the married families with Sergeant. T. Russell in charge, to sail to India.

When our train arrived at Tientsin we were received with rejoicing. As our barracks had now been taken over by the Somersets, the problem was where were we to be accommodated. Marching to the recreation ground, we pitched camp. Fortunately

Watching the battle in Han-K'ou from barricades in the Concessions

The Inniskillings disembark to return to guarding Tientsin

tents are always on hand here, in case of such an emergency. The advance party had all the needed equipment on the recreation ground by the time we arrived. It was now October and canvas was not the ideal accommodation for a Chinese winter: the month, however, was sunny and we were provided with plenty of blankets. We were in camp only a fortnight when a night's heavy rain turned our site into a miniature lake.

We awoke in the morning to find our kits and straw mattresses literally floating around the tents. To make matters worse, we had to

Adjourning for dinner, mess tins at the ready

Dinner, camp-style

endure a day of continuous rain with our clothes, bedding and kits in sodden condition. An emergency had arisen: we would have to clear away from this quagmire camp. Officials in the Concession were contacted and before evening temporary accommodation was provided in the Gordon Hall, Tientsin Club and various other buildings in the

The camp under water

Hutchinson's caption: 'They are
wet but happy'!

Concession. Many were lucky in getting fires going to dry their clothes
and bedding.

The Battalion was now scattered around the Concession and
remained so until a large go-down (store) was cleared and converted
into temporary barracks. This store was a three-storied building, with
hot and cold baths temporarily installed in the basement. It proved

fairly comfortable, though the ventilation was poor. It was here, I remember, that the first National Health Cards came into force (ninepence for fourpence).

China is well known for pirates, the criminal element being mostly composed of looting when trouble breaks out – as China is seldom free from strife this criminal element is very pronounced. As the rebel army advanced, law-abiding Chinese were in terror everywhere, owing to the criminal activities of these brigands. As organised government had ceased to exist, it was their opportunity to reap a good harvest. They raided and pilfered others, and roved the country villages to demand ransoms from village headmen, otherwise threatening to burn out the villages. The foreigners were not so much in fear of the opposing forces, but reckoned that the possibility of widespread looting was the real danger, shops and banks in the Concessions proving a greater prize than looting the poor natives. To the credit of the Rebel Forces, they did all in their power to curb the activities of looters, many hundreds of whom they shot or executed, even without trial. As the rebels advanced on Tientsin Native City fires broke out everywhere and practically the entire city was left in ruins. This of course was the work of looters as fire gave them the opportunity of grabbing and getting away. It was not the opposing armies so much that foreigners were afraid of, but looters, the banks and large shops especially, being most in danger.

Shot for looting in Tientsin[69]

---

[69] This and the following two photographs were not taken by Hutchinson, although he used them in his lantern slide lectures and included them in his album. He did not leave an indication of their source.

The troubles in Tientsin:
Chinese rush to leave the
burning city

Moving out goods and chattels
as fast as possible

On detachment in Wei-Hai-Wei

'B' Company under command of Captain Crawford went on detachment to Wei-Hai-Wei on 14 February 1912[70]. And at a later date 'C'

[70] It is interesting to speculate whether Hutchinson's path ever crossed with that of
Reginald F. Johnston, the Scot who was to become the famous tutor of the former Emperor,
P'u-Yi. Readers may recall Peter O'Toole's portrayal of Johnston in the film 'The Last
Emperor'. He served in the British colonial service as senior district officer for the South
Division of the Wei-Hai-Wei leasehold. He was there during Hutchinson's tour of duty,
although Hutchinson seems to have been assigned to a different district. Johnston
commented as follows about 1912: 'At the time when these great events were taking place in
Peking and Nanking, I was at Weihaiwei, where several distinguished Chinese loyalists were
glad to take refuge under the British flag, and where we had found it no easy task to convince

Company also left headquarters and were stationed at Feng-T'ai on the Imperial railway quite close to Peking. Doubtless to be at hand should the Legations there need their protection.

I was in 'B' Company. We embarked on a coastal steamer at Tientsin, sailed down the Pei-Ho River and into the Yellow Sea. We spent one night on board arriving in Wei-Hai-Wei harbour next day. The voyage out was fairly calm but on our return voyage the following autumn we experienced a rough passage. In fact it was the worst night that we ever endured at sea. Crockery was thrown all over the deck while every man clung unto something stable to avoid being washed overboard.

The bay at Wei-Hai-Wei

Wei-Hai-Wei in the province of Shan-Tung is situated in a bay which forms a splendid natural harbour. It was ceded to Britain in 1898 as a headquarters for our China fleet. A fourteen miles radius of the mainland around was also ceded as a protection to the harbour and islands. The natives living within this radius are actually British subjects. Our mission to Wei-Hai-Wei was to protect these subjects in the British territory on the mainland, especially from looters, also to control the influx of refugees from over the border.

We passed Chefoo town and harbour on our way down. When we arrived in Wei-Hai-Wei, a few British warships were anchored in the harbour. After dropping anchor, a ferry boat came alongside to take us and our baggage to the mainland where we occupied the barracks formerly built for and used by the now disbanded Wei-Hai-Wei Regiment. A very good barracks it was, but few of us were destined to enjoy it. After marching in and getting our kits into our quarters, the Company fell in to receive instructions etc as to why we were here and the duties to be carried out. After about a week, three sections under their commanders were allotted to outposts on the frontier. There were three outposts to be manned, one section remaining at

the 180,000 Chinese inhabitants of that territory that the emperor had indeed abdicated. For weeks their attitude was one of silent incredulity. Enthusiasm for the revolution was wholly lacking...' [Johnston, Reginald: *Twilight in the Forbidden City*, Victor Gollancz Ltd., London, 1934 (Oxford University Press reprint, 1985), page 89] headquarters. The outposts were situated about fourteen miles from Wei-Hai-Wei on the frontier and spaced around this radius. I was detailed with about twenty N.C.Os and men to occupy a position to the right of the radius, overlooking the sea, at Lou-Tao-Kiu village. The morning we set off was amusing if only for the primitive transport already waiting to take all our necessary equipment, stores etc. There were wheelbarrows, handcarts and even rickshaws with about ten coolies to draw them. To pack all our equipment including bedding, cooking utensils, coal, wood and ammunition on to this primitive transport was a problem that we left to the coolies who were more accustomed to loading their primitive conveyances than we were. We set off about 9 a.m. to cover this fourteen miles, the transport hauled by coolies in front while we marched behind. An interpreter accompanied us for without him the language problem could not be overcome. An interpreter was provided for each of the outposts. Fortunately a good road was at our disposal, made no doubt under British supervision. Between breakdowns and stops we eventually arrived at the bed of a river which flooded at high tides, within a mile of our destination. Here the road came to an abrupt end. In front of us was the river and beyond a waste of flat sand. To negotiate this river it was essential to unload, carry the vehicles across the river followed by the equipment and reload on the far side. The coolies were apparently accustomed to this sort of situation. They showed no hesitation to wade the river.

Coolies piggy-back the Inniskillings over the river

They set to on their task and in addition carried us across on their backs thus saving us the discomfort of wet clothing. Within an hour we were off again, the going for the coolies was much heavier in the soft sand.

Lou-Tao-Kiu village

We duly arrived in the village amidst excitement and curiosity. They were very friendly, as we had come to protect them. Three Wei-Hai-Wei police stationed in the temple were now a part of our garrison. Their knowledge of the district and people was a great help to me. Pushing on up the hill, the Buddhist temple was reached where we were to billet. Owing to the unsanitary condition of most Chinese villages, we were allowed to occupy the temple on a hill above. Strange place to live, amongst the idols.

Most temples, besides the joss houses where the idols are, consist of barn-like buildings. We cleared out two of these and made ourselves comfortable. The weather was becoming milder with summer approaching.

The detachment in Lou-Tao-Kiu, with the temple priest and two of the Wei-Hai-Wei police

All Buddhist temples in the interior of China are much alike. Built on hills and surrounded by groves. At our temple the grove had almost disappeared, having been cut down for firewood. The buildings consist of stable-like structures with a courtyard in the centre. Two gate idols stand guard on the entrance to ward off evil spirits. The joss house with its idols, altars and incense is like a horse stable, each horse box as it were containing an idol. We occupied three rooms or barns, one as a barrack room for the men, another for cooking etc while the third I used as a bunk and store for ammunition and medical supplies. The floors in all cases were mother earth. Windows were small, with glazed paper for glass. All temples are dark dismal places and this was no exception. The three native police stationed here occupied another room, my interpreter sharing quarters with them. We kept contact with the outpost on our left by visiting patrols sent out daily.

These police were the eyes and ears of the district. Being familiar with the inhabitants, they got all information regarding the situation both inside and outside the border, for the natives inside having relatives outside travelled to and fro. A message would occasionally come through by carrier from Wei-Hai-Wei that a wanted looter had escaped into the British territory. While we had no desire to get involved with the Chinese authorities outside, we were obliged either to capture such criminals and hand them over to our own authorities, or hustle them back over the border. Indeed, many a night in company with the police and interpreter we searched villages close to the frontier, receiving information that such criminals had relatives therein and were probably hiding there. The police would do the searching in the various houses while we stood on guard outside. Law and order was the function of the police, we being the authority and force behind them. We never succeeded in capturing any criminals. Usually when they heard that we were on their track they just cleared back again. We preferred not to capture them, only to ensure that they made their presence scarce in British Territory.

On many nights a reflection on the sky was a sure sign that a village was on fire. A sure sign also that a stream of refugees might be expected. On such nights we remained alert. A stream of Chinese lanterns approaching us over the border was the sign for us to intercept and allow the police to interview. Men with panic stricken womenfolk and children, some mounted on donkeys, others trudging aimlessly across country with all their belongings such as pots and pans etc, were a pitiful sight. Any having relatives were permitted to stay with them, provided the relatives were agreeable. Otherwise we passed them on to Wei-Hai-Wei. We forced none to return in case that doing so might involve loss of life. Chinese families, even in the British zone, were poor and to provide for relatives in this way was beyond the resources of most of them.

As the rebel army advanced [71] through our province of Shan-Tung, the noise of battle could be clearly heard. During this period we maintained patrols along the border to spot and report should our territory be invaded. Fortunately there were no incidents in this respect. Life was not monotonous: there were excitements nearly every night. During leisure hours we provided our own entertainment, if only assisting the two old priests in beating the drums and ringing bells to alert the idols for worship.

Chinese festivals were usually held on the first and fifteenth of each month or moon. On the night before a festival the temple would be lighted up with Chinese lanterns. The priests or caretakers, to alert the idols for worship next day would beat tom-tom drums and ring bells throughout the night. The troops enjoyed assisting, to the delight of the priest. Very early the following morning pilgrims would arrive to worship and burn incense in front of each idol. That ceremony over, counterfeit paper money would be burnt in a large stove-like contraption in the courtyard, an incense burner, the idea being to transmit money to their deceased ancestors.

Some of the men being of a musical disposition decided to form a band. They possessed a number of flutes and mouth organs. The old priest allowed them the use of his temple drums, so we had a band. It

Off duty in the temple compound, Lou-Tao-Kiu

[71] Bosworth comments that if indeed there was fighting in summer 1912, the 'rebels' could have been anti-republicans or simply bands of thieves or looters. The province of Shan-Tung had already gone over to the Republican cause in December 1911.

The detachment band at
Lou-Tao-Kiu

Carrying a load on the
bamboo pole

was great fun when they marched down the hill and through the village. The natives were highly amused for, apart from the village tom-tom and weird funeral pipes, they never heard music like this before. Drummer Davey Meehan was really the instigator of our band.

Captain Crawford our C.O. visited us periodically. On Fridays he brought our pay. He secured a grey horse to take him on visits to the three outposts. Money was of little use to us out here for there was nothing to spend it on. All our luxuries came from Wei-Hai-Wei with our daily supply of stores. An old Chinaman who must have reached the age of 65 carried out our stores each morning from Wei-Hai-Wei, a distance of fourteen miles. He would leave the Wei-Hai-Wei headquarters in the early hours and arrive with us about 8 a.m. With a bamboo pole over his shoulder and balanced with two sacks of stores, one at either end, he would jog along that fourteen miles and return again without a rest. We often heard of the endurance of the Chinese but this old man proved it. Sometimes to balance the load a boulder would be inserted in the lighter sack. I tried one morning to lift this burden on to my shoulder and found it was just as much as I could do. I would make a list out for any luxuries or extras needed by the men and give it to the old man, and same would be included in the following day's goods, the account being furnished by the grocer and paid weekly.

Being in possession of a sporting gun, I did plenty of shooting, for hare, geese, duck and teal were in abundance: they were roasted in a field oven which we built. Fortunately we had a good cook.

Corporal Hutchinson and colleagues board the train to leave Tientsin

The Inniskillings load their baggage at Ch'in-Huang-Dao

Besides keeping my men supplied with fresh meat while the season lasted, I managed to provide some for our staff in Wei-Hai-Wei.

In July, desiring to develop and print a lot of photographs and to make lantern slides, I asked permission to be allowed to change with another N.C.O. and return to headquarters, there being a suitable room in the old barracks. I found no difficulty in obtaining materials for a large store in Shang-Hai supplied me with everything necessary. It was here that I made most of my 600 slides.

Departure

We returned to Tientsin in October and joined our unit in the go-down. Preparations to leave Tientsin for India were now under way. It was in November 1912 that we entrained and left Tientsin for the last time, embarking on the troopship at Ch'in-Huang-Dao.

Postscript

AFTER about four days sail we reached Hong Kong. Here we disembarked and encamped for ten days on the mainland known as Kowloon opposite the island, whilst the transport underwent her periodical scraping etc in dry dock.

As members of the regiment with less than three years' service to complete their engagement were inadmissible to the Indian Government, a number of officers, N.C.Os and men left us at Hong Kong for the United Kingdom.

After a pleasant voyage we eventually arrived at Bombay in December. From Bombay we travelled for about two days by train over the Western Ghats. We reached Secunderabad[72] (Deccan) and marched to Meadows Barracks to spend our first Christmas in India. The families, parted from us a year earlier, awaited our arrival. Also a draft from the U.K., which came out to Deolali the previous year, did not join us until our arrival at Secunderabad. They were afterwards referred to as 'the Deolali draft'.

We found India very hot compared with north China. The barracks however were open and airy and during the very hot weather *punkhas* were employed to keep us cool at night. The mosquito and white ant were our worst enemies apart from the heat.

In October the following year Sergeant Modler and I went on six months' furlough in the U.K. Sergeant Modler got married and brought his bride out. Poor fellow was later killed at the Battle of the Somme in 1916.

Sergeant Modler and I returned to Secunderabad in March 1914. Shortly afterwards the battalion was re-organised, the former eight Company system being abandoned in favour of the present day four company and platoon system. The former Colour Sergeants were now known as Company Sergeant Major and Company Quarter Master Sergeant respectively. The choice of rank was left between the two Non Commissioned Officers of each double Company, wherever they were agreeable. Otherwise the ranks went by seniority, the senior being promoted to C.S.M. while the junior remained C.Q.M.S. or Company Accountant. Each Company was divided into 4 platoons with either a platoon officer or Sergeant in command, depending on the number of junior officers available. Subsequent training was

Corporal Hutchinson relaxes after his
endeavours

---

[72] Where Hutchinson assembled an album of 202 photographs from the north China assignment, presented to the Regimental Museum more than fifty years later.

The China Cup 'Presented to the 1st. Bn.,
Royal Inniskilling Fusiliers by the Irish
residents of Tientsin and Peking as a tribute to
the Regiment's service in protecting European
interests from the mutinous Chinese Army in
Northern China during the year 1911'
Courtesy, Regimental Museum of the Royal Inniskilling
Fusiliers, Enniskillen

intensified under this new formation. Major Jones assumed command in India, being promoted to Lt. Col., in place of Lt. Col. A. J. Hancocks who retired.

About this period Germany under the Kaiser was arming substantially and rumours of war were in the air. On August 4th 1914 war was declared with Germany, this causing great anxiety everywhere. Troops from India soon began to move for the U.K. We however still remained, only to move from Meadows Barracks to the fort at Trimulquerry close by, in about October.

As platoon officers were urgently needed throughout the Army, eligible N.C.Os who wished to apply for commissioned rank were requested to do so. Four or five of our senior N.C.Os were selected from the names submitted and subsequently transferred to home units. On the outbreak of war, many of our N.C.Os volunteered as instructors to our expanding forces and were sent to the United Kingdom. With vacancies occurring in this way, there were many promotions in the Battalion about this time.

Eventually about 15 December we left India, embarking at Bombay and sailing under escort for the U.K. We ate our Xmas dinner that year in Port Said harbour aboard the troopship. After a safe voyage in spite of enemy submarines, we duly arrived at Southampton early in January 1915. Travelling from there by train to an unknown destination, we finally arrived in Rugby where we were billeted on the inhabitants. After settling in, all ranks were given five days' leave. Many, including myself, got married while on this short furlough.

Intensive training was carried on at Rugby. Many units were now billeted in Birmingham, Coventry and many other cities and towns in Warwickshire. We were the only unit in Rugby. It was these units that subsequently formed the 29th Division.

Early in March tropical kit was issued. We were inspected by H.M. King George V near Daventry and on 16 March we left Rugby by train, destination unknown. Arriving at Avonmouth, we embarked on a troopship later and joined in convoy for the East. Disembarking at Alexandria, Egypt, we camped for about seven days, where we received preliminary training in landing technique, which gave us a clue that our mission was a landing on enemy territory.

On leaving Alexandria we sailed north, arriving in Lemnos harbour about 20th April. Here maps were produced and our mission explained. From this island officers and N.C.Os made a survey of Gallipoli about ten miles distant. We remained in Lemnos harbour for five days. We sailed out at midnight on 24th April. On Sunday morning 25th April 1915 at dawn, a landing was made on the Gallipoli peninsula. Our Navy commenced shelling the peninsula, *H.M.S. Queen Elizabeth* sending out broadsides from her 15 inch guns. The cliffs being manned with enemy machine guns, the landing was not as simple as we were led to believe. As the troopships had to remain a safe distance off shore, landing was made by lighters towed by naval pinnace under fierce machine gun and rifle fire. Heavy machine gun and rifle fire was encountered during landing operations. The *S.S. River Clyde*, specially prepared for her operation, was packed to capacity with troops and beached, the troops wading or swimming to shore. Casualties were heavy here, many being either shot or drowned.

This was our first taste of active service. It is not my purpose here[73] to continue this narrative on to our experiences on active service. Although few had experienced active service before, I am proud to mention that all ranks, mostly young, behaved splendidly under their 'baptism of fire'.

Despite the landing and subsequent advances, although we had many casualties, the battalion was fairly intact up to 22nd May. On that afternoon the Turks, under the command of German officers, made a fierce attack, undoubtedly to drive us into the sea, for we had our backs to the sea. Although the attack was held, our casualties in killed and wounded were heavy. A hand grenade or some other missile in close combat terminated my association with the battalion. With a shattered left arm, active service for me at all events had ended. It was at about this time that Sergeant Somers won his Victoria Cross[74].

After being 'patched up', then operated on in a hospital ship, I finally reached Southampton and thence by train to a hospital in Manchester. After about eight weeks in hospital I went on the usual leave and subsequently joined the Depot at Omagh. I remained at Omagh, being appointed for a time to No. 1 Company as C.Q.M.S. In March 1917 I volunteered for the permanent staff at the Command Depot, Tipperary, as C.Q.M.S. of No. 2 or "the Irish Company", consisting of Royal Munster Fusiliers, Connaught Rangers, Leinster Regiment and Royal Irish Regiment. In all over 1500 strong. My work and responsibilities were not light in a mixed company of such strength.

Although the war ended with the Armistice on 11 November 1918, I was retained to wind up the affairs of this Depot until May the following year when I received my final discharge.

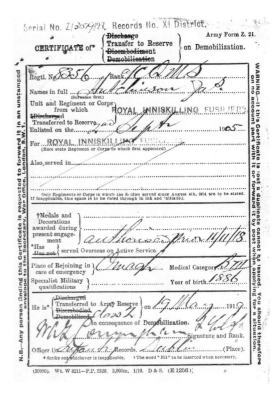

James Hutchinson's demob certificate

---

[73] See *The Dardanelles Campaign – A narrative of my adventures with the 29th Division in Gallipoli* by Sergeant J. Hutchinson (1st Battalion, The Royal Inniskilling Fusiliers), 1915. Published by Templar Press, Edmund Street, Birmingham.

[74] Sergeant James Somers won his VC on the night of July 1–2, 1915 in Gallipoli, when, owing to hostile bombing, some of the allied troops had retired from a sap, he remained alone there until a party brought up bombs. He then climbed over into the Turkish trench and bombed the Turks with great effect. Later on, he advanced into the open under heavy fire and held back the enemy by throwing bombs into their flank until a barricade had been established. During this period, he frequently ran to and from the allied trenches to obtain fresh supplies of bombs.

General index of English terms

CS = centre-spread

Aden 11, 15
Agriculture, Temple of 81
All Saints Church 40
Antrim, S.S. 1
Astor House Hotel 39
Astronomical Board 79, 80
Austria-Hungary 37, 57, 58

Bab-el-Mandeb 14
Belgium 30, 31, 43, 58, 90
Bell Tower 67, 68
Birds as pets CS, 72, 96, 97
Bitter Lake 10
Bleakley, Guy, R.S.M. 1, 4
Boxer Rising 28, 30, 38, 41, 43, 55, 59, 60, 61, CS, 65, 71, 89
Brazil 43
Bristow Road 40
Broken Column 41, CS
Bubonic plague 33
Buddha, Maitreya 66
Buddhism 63, 66, 74, 82, 87, 111, 112, 116, 133, 134
Buddhist Virtue, Temple of CS
Burnett, Sergeant Leo 5

Camels 11, 64, 95, 117, 118, 119
Canal du Jade 55
Canal Street 55, 57, 60
Candia 2, 3
Canea 2, 3
Cape Guardafui 15
Ceremonies, Book of 74
Ceylon 14, 15, 16
Chefoo 131
China Cup, The 140
China Seas 18
Chinese *passim*
Chinese Consular Service 59
Chou Dynasty 67, 87
Classics, Hall of 65
Climate (N. China) 27, 29, 30
Coal Hill 68, 71, 72
Colombo 16
Concession, Austro-Hungarian 30, 31
    Belgian 30, 31, 37
    British 30, 31, 37, 38, 40, 127 *et seq.*
    French 30, 31, 37, 40, 41
    German 30, 31, 37, CS
    Italian 30, 31, 37
    Japanese 30, 31, 37, 41, 60
    Russian 30, 31, 37, 41, 42

Confucius, Temple of 63, 65, 67, 82, 87, 102, 103
Connaught, H.R.H. Duke of 5, 6
Connor, D., Colour Sgt. 34
Cotton 45, 46, 47
Crete 2, 4
Cuba 57

Dalai Lama 83
Davidson, Lt. Col. C. J. L., D.S.O. 1, 33, 123
Denmark 57
Dragon, The 80
Drum Tower 68
Duffy, Private 32

East Mountain, Temple of 85
Ebrington Barracks 1
Education in China 100 *et seq.*
Edward VII, H.M. King 6, 33
Eighteen Hells, Temple of 86, 87
Elgin, Lord 111
Emperor of Germany 6
Empress Dowager Ci-Xi 71, 73, 123
English Chinese Engineering and 40
Mining Company
Eternity, Mountain of 111
Examination Hall 103

Favier, Bishop 71
First World War 35, 141 *et seq.*
Forbidden City 54, 64 *et seq.*
Framingham, C. Sgt/R.S.M. 4
France 4, 38, 41
French troops 32, 35

Gallagher, Sergeant 35
Gallipoli 141
Genghis Khan 116
George V, H.M. King 121, 140
German contingent 35
Germany 6, 37, 38, 60, CS, 65, 89, 140
Gibraltar 2
Goddess of Mercy 83 *et seq.*, 87
God of Riches 84
Gods of Work 85
Good Templars, International 7
Order of
Gordon Hall, The 38
Gorman, Sergeant F. 33
Grand Canal 44, 50, 72
Grave mounds 28, 119
Great Felicity, Gate of 73
Great Felicity, Hall of 73
Great Wall, The 109, 113 *et seq.*, 121
Greece 2

Hancocks, Lt-Col. A. J. 123, 124
Hanlin Academy 55
Heavenly Peace, Gate of 73
Hedjaz 14
Hohenzollern, yacht 6
Hong Kong 19, 21 *et seq.*, 27, 123, 139
Horse Street 44

Idols 64, 75, 82, 84, 87
Imperial Canal 55
Imperial Chair 78
Imperial City 54, 67, 69, 70, 75, 80
Imperial Civil Service examination 102 *et seq.*
Imperial Railway 24 *et seq.*, 51, 55, CS, 75, 113, 122, 131
Imperial Summer Palace CS, 109 *et seq.*
Imtarfa Barracks 5
India 14, 23, 40, 43, 66, 107, 112, 125 *et seq.*, 138 *et seq.*
Indian barbers 36
Indian Ocean 15 *et seq.*
Industrial Meeting Grounds 45
Inner City, Peking 63
International/Liberation Bridge 41
Irkutsk 114
Irwin, Corporal C. 5, 6
Italy 2, 37, 57, 60, 71

Japan 23, 26, 30, 31, 37, 39, 41, 45, 51, 57, 60, 111
Johnston, Reginald F. 131
Jones, Major/Lt. Col. 124, 140
Jubal, Straits of 13

Kalgan 113 *et seq.*
von Ketteler, Baron 65, 66
von Ketteler Memorial 65, 66
Kiakhta 114
Kirkpatrick, Lieut. 34, 124
Knossos 4
Kow-tow 80
Krupp Iron Works 39

Lake Menzaleh 10
Lama Temple 63 *et seq.*, 70, 83
Lascars 12
Legation Guards 56, 59
Legation Quarter 55 *et seq.*, 64, 69
Legation, American 57, 58, 61
    Austro-Hungarian 57, 58
    Belgian 57, 58
    British 56 *et seq.*
    French 57, 59
    German 57, 59, 61

Italian 57, 60
Japanese 57, 60
Mexican 60
Netherlands 60
Portuguese 57, 60
Russian 57, 59
Spanish 57, 60
de Lesseps, Ferdinand 10
Liaoning, Province 26
Liberation/International Bridge 41
Liscum, Col. Emerson H. 41
Lohan, disciples of Buddha 66, 112
Lunn, Lance Corporal 6

Maguire, Provost/C. Sgt/Major 4
Mahomedans 2, 14, 63, 79, 90, 104, 107
Malacca, Straits of 17
Malta 2, 4 *et seq.*, CS
Manchuria 44, 109, 114
Marco Polo 116
Meadows Road 40
Meehan, Davey, Drummer 137
Mencius 63, 67, 102
Meyer-Waldeck, Alfred 60
Midday Sun, Gate of 73
Military Attachés 56, 58, 59
Ming Dynasty 50, 54, 64, 68, 71, 74, 109 *et seq.*
Modler, Sergeant 139
Mongol Dynasty 50, 54, 112, 116
Mongolia 23, 44, 66, 114 *et seq.*
Mongolians 52
Mooshedagerah 14
Morris, W. A., Lt. & Q.M. 124, 126
Moukden 27
Mount Sinai 11
Municipal Library 38
Myriad Buddhas, Temple of CS, 111

Nanking 130
Native City 30, 37, 42 *et seq.*
Netherlands 60
New Territories 21

Observatory 90
Omagh 1, 141
Order, Gate of 73
Outer City 54

P & O Steamship Company 9
Pei-T'ang Cathedral 70, 71
Peking 24, 27, 30, 44, 50 *et seq.*, 96, 100 *et seq.*, 109 *et seq.*, 121 *et seq.*, 140

Penitential Fasting, Hall of 76, 78, 79
Perim 14, 15
Phoenix, The 80
Phosphorescence 15
Photography 4, 6, 138, 139
Pidgin English 105 *et seq.*
Pike, Captain 123
Pirates 23 *et seq.*
Populations 30, 41, 49, 52, 54, 72, 90
Port Arthur 26
Port Said 9 *et seq.*
Precious Mountain pagoda 112
Precious Ones, The 87
Prince Regent 73
Punjabi Regiment 29, 34

Quai du Congrès 55

Red Sea 10 *et seq.*
Revolution of 1912 125, 131
Rickshaws 32, 41, 48, 62 *et seq.*, 90
Rites, Board of 80
Rockhill, Mr. 52
Roland 38
Royal Army Temperance Association 5, 7
Royal Garrison Artillery 2
Russell, Sergeant 126
Russia 2, 26, 30 *et seq.*, 37, 41, 42, 57, 59, 111, 116

St Andrew's Barracks 4, 5
St. Louis Roman Catholic Church 40
St Patrick's Day 33
Sardinia, S.S. 6
Sea of Wisdom, Temple of 111
Secunderabad 139
Shadwan 13
Shanks, Private Samuel 121
Sicilia, Hired Transport 2
Singapore 17 *et seq.*
Small Water Gate 52, 55, 58
Smythe, R. C. Captain, Adjutant 1, 123
Socotra 15
Soddhodana, King of Kapila 81
Somali, Hired Transport 125
Somers, Sergeant, V.C. 141
Somerset Light Infantry 125, 126
Soudan, Hired Transport 9, 26
Sports 2, 5, 32, 33, 121
Steadfast Purity, Gate of 73
Steadfast Purity, Palace of 73
Stevenson, Private 5

Suez Canal 9 *et seq.*, 14, 14
Sullivan, Lieut. 34
Sumatra 17
Sweden 57

Taiping Rebellion 38
Taoism 74, 82, 85
Tartars 54, 72, 74
Tartar City 52 *et seq.*, 63 *et seq.*, 68, 69, 73, 75, 89, 90
Temple of Heaven 54, 64, CS, 68, 74 *et seq.*
Thirteen Tombs, The 119
Thomann, Commander 58
Three Oceans 69
Throne Hall 73
Tibet 44, 66, 67, 114
Tientsin 9, 24 *et seq.*, 37 *et seq.*, 50 *et seq.*, CS, 114, 121 *et seq.*, 137, 140
Tientsin Club 39
Tientsin, Native City 37, 43
Tientsin, Victoria Park 38
Tipperary 141
Tramway, Hong Kong 20, 21, 22
Trans-Siberian Railway 27, 51, 114
Treaty Temple 39
Trimulquerry 140
Trooping the Colour 34
Turkey 2, 141

Union Church 40
United States of America 30, 31, 41, 47, 52, 57, 58, 61, 114, 124
Urga 114

Valletta 4, 5
Verbiest, Father, SJ 90
Verdella Barracks 4 *et seq.*
Victoria Barracks 1

Wagons-Lits Hotel 57, 60, 61
Walls, Peking 52, 54, 55, 61, 64, 72, 76
White Clouds, Temple of 111, 112
Winter Palace 69, 70

Yamato Koen Park 41
Yellow River 25, 26
Yellow Sea 25, 26, 131
Yellow Temple 83
Yuan Dynasty 89, 116

Zanzibar 13
Zoological and Botanical Gardens 90

Index of Chinese proper names
(*approximate Wade-Giles orthography*)

Canton 20, 21
Chai-Kung 78
Chia-Ching, Emperor 71
Ch'ien-Ch'ing-Kung 73
Ch'ien-Ch'ing-Men 73
Ch'ien-Lung, Emperor 67, 74, 83, 119
Ch'ien-Men Gate 73, 75, 90
Ch'ien-Men Street 58, 69, 81
Ch'ien-Men Terminus 75
Chihli Province 44
Chi-Hui-Hai 111
Ch'ing-Ho 113
Ch'ing-Lung-Ch'iao 113, 117
Ching-Shan/Mei-Shan 68, 71, 72
Ch'in-Huang-Dao 26, 27, 44, 121 *et seq.*,
    137, 138
Ch'i-Nien-Tien 75, 79
Chun, Prince, Prince Regent 73
Chung-Ho-Tien 73
Chu-Yung-Kuan 114, 116

Feng-shui 65
Feng-T'ai 75
Fo-Hsiang-Ko CS, 111

Guangxu, Emperor 73

Hai-Guang-Ssu 41
Hai-Ho/Haihe River 28, 44, CS
Hata-men Gate 55, 61 *et seq.*
Hong 38
Hong-Kong 19 *et seq*, 123, 139
Hsi-An-Men Gate 69
Hsi-Chi-Men Gate 90
Hsiao-Shui-Men 52, 55, 58
Hsi-Ku 67
Hsi-Ling 72
Hsiang-Shan 112
Hsuan-wang, Emperor 100
Huang-Ch'iung-Yu 75, 79
Huang-Ho River 25, 26

K'ang-Hsi, Emperor 75

Kowloon 20, 21
Kuang-An-Men 83
Kuan-Te-Tien 72
Kublai Khan 54, 89
Kun-Ming-Hu 112
Kwang-Hsu, Emperor 75
Kwan-yin, goddess 83, 84, 87

Liaoning, Province 26
Li-Hung-Chang, Viceroy 37, 39, 45
Lou-Tao-Kiu 132 *et seq.*
Lu-an-men 73
Lueshun 26
Lu-Tai Canal 44

Ma-Lu 44
Miaoying Monastery 73
Moukden 27

Nan-K'ou 109 *et seq.*
Nei-Ch'eng 63, 73

Pai-T'ai 75
Pa Kua 82
Pao-Ho-Tien 73
Pao-Kuo-Ssu 83
Pa-Ta-Ling 113 *et seq.*
Pei-chi-li, Gulf of 26
Pei-Ho, River 28, 30, 37, 41, 44
Pei-Tai-Ho/Beidaihe 114
P'u-Yi, Emperor 130

San Hai 71
San-Kwan-Miao 72
Sha-Ho 113
Shang-hai 25, 138
Shang-Shu-Fang 73
Shan-Hai-Kwan 114, 115
Shantung 25, 85, 131
Shi-Fei-Ssu 114
Shi-Huang-Ti, Emperor 114
Shih-San-Ling 119
Shun-Chi, Emperor 75

Shun-Chi-Men 64, 90
Sun-Yat-Sen 123, 124
Sze-Chu-Lin 37

Ta-Ch'ing-Men Gate 69, 73
T'ai-Ho-Men 73
T'ai-Ho-Tien 73
T'ai-Shan, mountain 85
Tai-Shui-Tien 81
Taku, Bar 29
Taku Forts 28
T'angshan 28
Tien-An-Men 73
Tientsin 9, 24 *et seq.*, 37 *et seq.*, 50 *et seq.*,
    CS, 114, 121 *et seq.*, 137, 140
Tuan Ch'i-jui (Duan Qirui) 60
Tung-An-Men Gate 69
Tung-Ling 72
Tung-Yueh-Miao 85
Tu-Teng 112
Tz'u-hsi/Ci-Xi, Empress Dowager 71, 73,
    123

Wai-Wu-Pu 111
Wan-Li-Ch'ang Ch'eng 115
Wan-Shou-Shan 111, 113
Wan-Wan-Sui-Yeh 82
Wei-Hai-Wei 44, 87, 130 *et seq.*
Wu-Kwei-T'ou 114
Wu-men 73

Yamen 59, 60, 64, 111
Yang-Hsin-Tien 73
Yang-Tse-Kiang, River 25
Yi-Ho-Yuan 111
Yin-Yang 82
Yuan Shikai 124
Yung-Cheng, Emperor 66, 67
Yun-Hui-Ssu 112
Yung-Lê 64, 68, 119, 120

Zhangjiakou 113